Cycling Kenya

Biking and Hiking Safaris in the African Paradise

Kathleen Bennett

Bicycle Books — San Francisco

Printed in the United States of America

Cover design Kent Lytle
Cover photograph The Image Bank

Except where credited differently, all photographs by the author

Published by:
Bicycle Books, Inc.
PO Box 2038
Mill Valley, CA 94941 (USA)

Distributed to the Book Trade by:
USA: National Book Network, Lanham, MD
UK: Chris Lloyd Sales and Marketing Services, Poole, Dorset
Canada: Raincoast Book Distribution, Vancouver, BC

Publisher's Cataloging in Publication Data:

Bennett, Kathleen, 1943—
Cycling Kenya: Biking and Hiking Safaris in the African Paradise.
Series Title: Active Travel Series
Bibliography: p.
1. Travel, guidebooks and manuals
2. Kenya, guidebooks and manuals
3. Bicycles and cycling, tour guides
4. Authorship
I. Title
Library of Congress Catalog Card Number: 91-77703
ISBN: 0-933201-42-7 paperback original

DEDICATION

This book is dedicated to the friends who encouraged me to write, each in his own special way. My sincere thanks...

to **Gary**, who more than anyone else believed I could and should write;

to **Michael**, who gave me and my word processor a home in Nairobi;

to **Hugh**, who first taught me the rewards of bicycle touring;

to **Terry**, who led me on long walks in the Colorado mountains;

to **Lloyd**, who is always a supportive friend; and

to **Dick**, who shared with me his heart and his love for adventure.

"Kenya's climate and variety make it challenging cycling country and if it appeals to you — whether you're a lycra-laminated pro or just use a bike once in a while — it's one of the best ways of getting around."

Richard Trillo, <u>The Rough Guide to Kenya</u>

"Walking (...) is highly recommended and gives you unparalleled contact with local people." "With a bike and a tent, once again, you can go anywhere in Kenya. Traditional touring machines will cope on most tar and dirt roads without any trouble... Carrying bikes on buses is no problem, and useful if long uninteresting sections need to be crossed... The lakeside roads south-west of Kisumu, or the Cherangani Mountains are among many ideal mountain bike routes."

David Else, <u>Camping Guide to Kenya</u>

"The bicycle, he said, was shared between himself and his partner. If both young men wanted to visit the town together, they took it in turns to walk and ride. One went ahead on the bicycle, left it ten miles along the road and proceeded on foot. The second walked the first ten miles, found the bicycle, and caught up his friend. In this way they reached Nairobi, a distance of fifty miles, in one day. No one ever molested the bicycle, which they had bought second-hand for ten rupees."

Elspeth Huxley, <u>The Flame Trees of Thika</u>

Kathleen Bennett moved to Kenya in 1988 from La Jolla, California, where she worked as an English Instructor at San Diego Mesa College. While flying to Europe to interview for a job in Switzerland, she watched the movie *Out of Africa*. Although this was the third time she had seen the movie, this showing signaled her future. Before she returned to California, a contract to teach in Kenya had been signed.

In addition to her travels throughout East Africa by bicycle and on foot, Ms. Bennett has cycled and trekked through many European countries, as well as New Zealand, South America, Guatemala, Baja California, Australia, and the United States. She is single and usually travels alone, occasionally joined by her son Troy and her daughter Shannon.

She believes that once you have known Africa and its people well, there is no turning back (to live exclusively in the West). Residing in Kenya has fulfilled many of her adventurous dreams.

In 1986, after reading Alan Paton's book *You Can Have It All*, Ms. Bennett's lifestyle underwent a dramatic change. She sold her home and real estate business in Colorado, resolving to seek what she loved best — adventures in far-off places. Now, as a professional writer and vagabond, spending most of her time traveling in East Africa, she feels that she truly does 'have it all.'

Introduction

"I think I shall always stick to my bike," said Christopher. "The bicycle is the most civilized conveyance known to man. Other forms of transport grow daily more nightmarish. Only the bicycle remains pure in heart."
Iris Murdoch, <u>The Red and the Green</u>, 1965

Kenya has given the world its word for journey — *safari*. To go on safari in the early years of this century was a costly and complicated undertaking. When Teddy Roosevelt set off from Nairobi's Norfolk Hotel during his sporting visits, a hundred porters would follow, carrying sufficient supplies for several months in the bush.

Over the years, safaris have become increasingly easier — too easy in fact. Better roads and 4-wheel drive vehicles have popularized brisk travel through Kenya. Today, tourists are whisked from one national park to another, sadly eliminating the real adventure of safari life. Limited contact with the people, land, and animals have made a safari a predictable and rather superficial experience.

Fortunately, the uniqueness of the wildlife and the glory of the landscape have not changed. Many tribes have retained their ancient traditions and lifestyles. In short, the real Africa still exists and is easily accessible.

Safe adventurous safaris in Kenya are within everyone's grasp. No doubt the elaborate safaris of Roosevelt's era are over; both hunting and the sale of game trophies were banned in the late 1970's. Today it is only the active travelers exploring Kenya by bicycle and on foot who still realize the genuine closeness to the land and the people that these early safari-seekers prized.

Adventurous Safaris Today

When I moved to the Kenyan town of Thika in 1988, a mountain bike and hiking shoes were with my luggage. During the first six months there, no one I met owned a bicycle or showed the least interest in cycling and walking excursions. At even the mere suggestion, most foreign residents scoffed that traveling through Kenya without a car was a crazy idea.

After several months of touring with others by car, I had no in-depth understanding of the people, the animals or the landscape visited. While staring through car windows at many interesting sights, I had experienced practically nothing. This distressed me greatly. After moving halfway around the world with hopes of gaining a rich perspective of this African culture, I was dissatisfied. Traveling by car had isolated me from the local people, their country, and the likelihood of any adventures.

An immediate change in my style of safari was called for. I decided to slow down and put myself in contact with the land and the people. I wiped six months of dust off my bicycle and hiking boots and set off.

When I cycled and walked through the same mountains and savannas I had previously whizzed through by car, the difference was phenomenal. The sights and sounds, the very rhythm of Africa began to come alive. I traveled alone, and the dangers my concerned advisers had warned me about simply never materialized. My new friends were Pokot tribesmen from the Cherangani Hills, Masai morans from the Rift Valley, and Meru farmers from the slopes of Mt. Kenya.

Once the spectacular beauty of this culture has been really experienced it casts a spell over those who have dared to depart from the typical tourist trail. Amidst volcanoes still smoldering from recent acts of creation, survive wild animals and primitive tribes. A sense of man's origin lingers on. By the end of a cycling or walking safari, the Kikuyu's belief that God lives on the peak of Mt. Kenya will seem less implausible. One is forever changed by the discovery of the strange and marvelous mystique pervading this equatorial paradise.

Table of Contents

Part I
General Information

CHAPTER 1

Cycling and Walking in Kenya

"He was himself at heart also a romantic, drawn to Africa less by a dream of fortune than by a wish for freedom (. . .) His Sundays were spent walking about the plains and hills in search of lions and buffaloes."
  Elspeth Huxley, *The Flame Trees of Thika*, 1959

A cycling and walking safari in Kenya is a supreme adventure and delight available to anyone, regardless of age and fitness. The country is a veritable panoply of peoples, wildlife, and

This book makes safe and adventurous safaris available to everybody. May you leave Kenya knowing that you have truly ventured 'on the wild side.' (photo Major Aussie Walker)

11

geography — all accessible. Yet most visitors hurry through Kenya's national parks by car in search of the 'Big Five,' sadly missing the immense diversity of music, art, and life that lies beyond.

The real Africa is found in the areas seldom visited by tourists. To get there requires a little extra effort and planning, but the rewards are abundant. Journeying in sync with the pulse of the continent is the only way to get the most out of a safari experience. This means slowing down and fine-tuning all the senses. Like precious old wine, Kenya should be savored. Its complexities are many. The Great Rift Valley stretches below the snowy peaks of Mt. Kenya. Overhead the swishing sounds of giant cranes drown distant chants of Masai herdsmen. Zebra and giraffe graze silently by the roadside. Such wonders are frequent, though never commonplace, for those who cycle and walk through Kenya.

The belief that Kenya is a dangerous place for active travelers is a myth that needs shattering. Quite the contrary is true. This country abounds with safe and scenic routes, and visitors quickly discover the warmth and hospitality of its people.

Many benefits result from touring on bicycle and foot. Close contact with the land and people is established. Making friends with locals, who come from a cultural potpourri of 52 tribes, is relaxed and unforced. Departing from the typical tourist trail and getting in touch with the African landscape precipitates adventures. Cyclists and walkers develop keen senses as more detail is observed, unlike isolated car tourists who spot large animals through car windows. Far greater numbers of the smaller animals and birds are seen. Most remarkably, tranquillity is attained by those who establish a connection with the wild, and the walls that civilization has built between Man and Nature are broken down.

Freedom and flexibility are two superb bonuses of a cycling and walking safari. The most memorable times during holidays are frequently those that are unplanned. The freedom to stop at will and to rearrange daily plans is important. When spontaneous opportunities occur, simply apply the brakes and dismount. Liberated travel comes with the flexibility to create schedules and to modify them. Escaping crowds and the boring rituals of visiting endless 'tourist traps' are easily forgone.

Active travel is stimulating. Challenging the body and brain can do wonders for mental health, not to mention physical health and fitness.

After cycling from Dunkirk to Delhi, travel-writer Dervla Murphy summarized the benefits of active journeys:

"At least one exerts oneself cycling and the speed is not too outrageous and one is constantly exposed to the elements."

Lucky indeed are travelers who pedal along scenic roads and walk over uncongested trails, for they soon discover the heart of Africa, as old and mysterious as giant baobob trees.

How This Book Helps Active Travelers

This guide book aims to assist all outdoor enthusiasts by organizing their safaris throughout Kenya. To simplify planning, the country is divided into six touring regions. Long cycling tours and short loops are rated according to distance and difficulty of the terrain. Security and health precautions are detailed, and equipment checklists are provided. Lodging, camping, and eating establishments, as well as sidetrips by foot, dhow, canoe, steamer, and horse are suggested. Finally, descriptive maps, which can be photocopied and conveniently fit into a bicycle handlebar bag, are certain to keep everyone heading in the desired direction.

The chief goal of this book is to make safe, adventurous safaris available to everyone. Despite this practical focus, I

The author riding amongst giraffes at Giraffe Manor in the Nairobi suburb of Karen. (photo Richard Hartley)

Watching 2.1 million flamingos nesting at the edge of Lake Bogoria in the Great Rift Valley.

trust that my fascination with Kenya is not obscured. The three years I have lived in this multifaceted land have been deeply rewarding. As you select routes and make equipment choices, my hope is that you also begin to sense the extraordinary beauty of the country soon to be encountered.

May you leave Kenya knowing that you have truly ventured 'on the wild side.'

CHAPTER 2

Safaris for Everyone

"A London doctor who took to doing his rounds on a bicycle because it was more pleasant, healthier, more economical of energy and did not pollute the air, decided that the future might well belong to Cycling Man."
  Ronald E. Williams, *British Medical Journal*, 1975

Cycling and walking safaris are for everyone in reasonably good health (if uncertain, check with a doctor) who enjoys exercise and can ride a bicycle. Selecting an itinerary suited to particular age and fitness levels takes only a few hours of planning. Tour options are available for the experienced and novice, the budget and luxury, and the highly adventurous and somewhat conservative traveler. Families with small children and grandparents need not miss out. Short rides and walks, included in family holiday plans, become the most valued memories of Africa.

Mt. Longonot is one of more than thirty dormant volcanoes in Kenya's Great Rift valley. A walk to the crater rim takes two hours, and to circle the rim another two. See Rift Valley Wonders Grand Tour in Chapter 16.

Remember that fitness enthusiasts, like ice cream, come in a variety of distinct flavors. Each is special in his or her own way. For this reason the tours in this book are rated according to three levels of difficulty: *Easy*, *Challenger*, and *Hardcore*.

☐ **Easy** routes cover mostly flat terrain and short distances, usually 5–25 miles (8–40 km). The roads may not always be paved, but they are suitable for inexperienced cyclists or those desiring gentle rides.

☐ **Challenger** routes include hills interspersed with flat terrain and longer distances, about 25–60 miles (40–95 km). Road conditions are variable, including some rough, rocky stretches suitable for competent riders with good cycling skills who are ready for some challenges.

☐ **Hardcore** routes are for those who are not intimidated by mountains, long distances of 60–120 miles (95–190 km), and rough roads. Only experienced cyclists should undertake Hardcore routes, though strong Challengers may find themselves advancing to Hardcore levels. At times the only difference between a Hardcore and Challenger route is the distance covered.

If you are consistently active and confident of your fitness and cycling abilities, you will likely select Challenger and Hardcore tours. If you exercise only sporadically and are unsure of your endurance, you should start with the less strenuous Easy tours.

Short, Long, and Moderate Safaris

Short Tours: Combining active outings with traditional car safaris.

Limitations of time are the most problematic thorns bursting the bubble of many vacationers' dreams. Even those with time constraints can sample some of the shorter loops lasting only a few hours or days. After reading the Overviews describing the six touring regions, identify the locale you want to observe most closely.

Spending some time cycling and walking is a welcome break from the traditional car-safari routine. Bouncing over rough roads in confining vehicles becomes tiring after a few days. Exercise provides freedom and a much needed change-of-pace. After photos of the 'Big Five' have been secured during game park drives, try adventuring a few hours or days in this unconfining style. (See the section *Organized Tours* in Chapter 3, *Pre-Trip Planning*.)

☐ **Grand Tours:** Traveling exclusively by bicycle and on foot. An extensive tour of Kenya traveling exclusively on bicycle and foot is definitely possible. If good fortune has blessed you with all the time in the world, let the wind blow you in the direction of any or all the Grand Tours. Each region is endowed with spectacular scenery and cultural diversity. Grand Tours have their challenging moments indeed. However, bypassing any part of the route is accomplished by using one of the public transportation options.

☐ **Moderate Tours:** Using motor vehicle support. Those desiring a moderate approach to active travel operate under the motto 'Bike and hike the best; use transport for the rest.' Why not select specific areas you genuinely want to take time to savor? Afterwards use public

Trains make two daily runs between Nairobi and Kenya's coast. The afternoon train passes through Nairobi National Park. (photo Major Aussie Walker)

transportation or a hired car to carry you, your bicycle, and your luggage to the next destination.

Six Transportation Options for Bicycles, Luggage, and Riders

Transportation for people and equipment is not scarce in Kenya. Buses and *matatus* (collective minibuses) are found practically everywhere. They are cheap, though a small extra fee is usually charged for luggage. Frequently crowded and lively, *matatus* offer bountiful opportunities to meet more local people. However, you must be willing to ride in some discomfort.

Hitchhiking is probably much safer in Kenya than in many Western countries. Common sense dictates that it is usually better to accept rides with families, especially if traveling solo. Offer to pay when hitching. Gasoline is expensive, and it is considered good manners by locals to pay for this service.

The most popular train rides from Nairobi are east to Mombasa and west to Kisumu, although the train also travels northwest to Eldoret and south to Taveta. Anyone who has read the history of Kenya's 'Lunatic Express' will want to hop aboard for at least one trip. Kenya Airways is the national airline and, within Kenya, flies to Malindi, Mombasa, Kisumu, and Nairobi. Private airlines, based at Nairobi's Wilson Airport, service the national parks, Lake Turkana, and smaller cities.

Finally, hiring a car with a driver is an inexpensive option if a group shares the costs. Cars can be rented for about 500 KS per day (US $22, UK £16) plus mileage. Drivers are paid 200 KS per day plus accommodation and meals. A rental car can be used as a 'sagwagon,' carrying luggage and tired riders to the next destination.

CHAPTER 3

Pre-Trip Planning

*"Is it lack of imagination that makes us come to imagined places,
not just stay at home? Or could Pascal have been not entirely
right about just sitting quietly in one's room?*
   Elizabeth Bishop, Questions of Travel, 1970

Climate

Deciding when to visit Kenya is a less important consideration
than with most other destinations. Weather in this equatorial
country is pleasant year-round. The north and low-lying coast
remain hot while the highlands are usually warm or mild.
However, in late February and March along the Coast, high
humidity and temperatures above 90° F (32° C) can make
strenuous exercise uncomfortable.

    The pattern of rainy and dry seasons is what most concerns
cyclists and walkers. Rainy months customarily are April and
May at the Coast and between March and September in the
Western Highlands. In the Eastern Highlands and Nairobi, the

*Luxury organized tours provide bicycles, sagwagon, and all the
necessary gear.*

19

long rains fall between March and June with short rains in November. To further complicate matters, the rainy seasons have been erratic during recent years; rain has come during months which were formerly dry and vice versa. Locals believe that the rainy seasons are changing. They may be right, but trying to outguess Mother Nature has always been a tricky business.

Do not let the predicted rainy months deter travel plans. Rains rarely occur everyday. When they do arrive, these showers or downpours last only a few hours, leaving a glistening, freshly-washed landscape for cycling and walking.

Everyone can find a climate in Kenya to make him or her feel alive and energetic. If cool breezes invigorate you, head for the Aberdares or Cherangani Hills. If you need to thaw out after a cold winter at home, go straight to Lake Magadi or the Coast. Conversely, if you have always dreamed of throwing snowballs on the equator, Mt. Kenya's peaks can amply supply the ammunition for this fantasy. The variety of climates Kenya offers is a delightful discovery for many visitors, who usually expect a tropical and hot climate throughout Africa.

Necessary Paperwork

Getting all necessary paperwork in order is the least fun, but most necessary task of pre-trip planning. Review this checklist to determine if every required document has been secured.

Paperwork Checklist

1. Valid passport. Check that yours is current.

2. Visa for Kenya. US citizens must possess a visa. Those exempted are citizens of the Commonwealth, West Germany, Denmark, Finland, the Netherlands, Norway, Sweden, Spain, Uruguay, Ethiopia, and Turkey, who may enter with a Visitor's Pass. Regulations change, so check with the nearest Kenya High Commission to learn current visa requirements.

3. International Vaccination Certificate. Verification of yellow fever and cholera may be required. Personnel at the Immunization Centre of Jomo Kenyatta Airport, Nairobi, have stated that visitors arriving from Europe, North America, or Australia are not required to show proof of these vaccinations. Frankly, I would rather have the proof than take a chance of getting stopped at Immigration.

Getting a Visa

For those who have not previously traveled to countries requiring visas, the procedure for obtaining one may be hazy.

Time: Obtaining a visa should take only two or three days if you apply in person at a Kenya High Commission. If this is impossible, allow five to seven working days. To save time, use express mail one-day service if this is available where you live, including a prepaid receipt for the return posting by express mail.

Forms: Larger tourist agencies can supply you with the necessary forms to apply for a visa. If these are unavailable, request the necessary forms directly from a Kenya High Commission or Kenya Tourist Office.

In the USA, call or write to one of the following:
○ Kenya Tourist Office, 9100 Wilshire Blvd., Doheny Plaza, Suite 111, Beverly Hills, CA 90212. Telephone (213) 274-6634/5
○ Kenya Embassy, 2249 R. Street NW, Washington, DC 20008. Telephone (202) 387-6101

In the UK, call or write:
○ Kenya High Commission, 45 Portland Place, London, W1N 4AS. Telephone (071) 636-2371.

Photos: Obtain two clear passport-size pictures from a professional store. The photo-booth variety is often unacceptable. Shop around for a photography service that will give you the negative with several prints. Having this negative means that extra copies will cost little in the future.

Fees: Before mailing or delivering the visa forms, passport, and photos, do not forget to include the required fees. Personal checks are not always acceptable. The form will indicate the amount and method of payment required.

Visas Upon Arrival in Kenya

Visas can be obtained at the Jomo Kenyatta International Airport in Nairobi if you arrive by air. I have personally secured a Kenya Visa in this way, although several guidebooks state erroneously that this option is not available.

It is always best to acquire your visa prior to travel. If for some reason you cannot secure a visa in advance, you may encounter a long line at the Nairobi International Airport visa counter.

Organized Cycling and Walking Tours

The decision to join an organized group or travel independently is largely a matter of personal preference, although other factors may influence this decision. Consider these reasons for joining an organized cycling or walking tour:

☐ **Time Limitations.** Either vacation days are limited, or busy schedules preclude having time for the necessary planning.

☐ **Worry-free.** Vacations can mean freedom from major decision-making. Tours can be arranged whereby others can handle luggage and make decisions for accommodations, meals, and sightseeing.

☐ **Company.** Some people do not like traveling alone, or they feel less secure without knowledgeable leaders around. For socially-oriented travelers, the group experience can be great fun.

Organized tours currently available last several hours or weeks. Some are budget-conscious; others are more luxurious. A few cater to hardcore cyclists or technical climbers, while most are geared for slow and moderate participants. Survey the organized tour options listed below. Check for more organized trips in recent issues of *Outside, Backpacker, The Adventurers, Bicycling, Specialty Travel Index, Great Expeditions,* and other magazines focusing on active travel.

Organized Bicycle Safaris

- *Paradise Bicycle Tours, Inc.* PO Box 1726, Evergreen, CO 80439, USA. Tel. (303) 670-1842. Specializing in 15-day camping and luxury tours, and 3–5 day outings with vehicle support. Bicycles, helmets, gloves furnished.
- *Bicycle Africa.* 4887 Columbia Drive South, Seattle, WA 98108. Tel. (206) 767-3927. Budget 14–21 day tours. No vehicle support. Bicycles available or use your own.
- *Bike Treks.* P.O. Box 14237, Nairobi, Kenya. Tel. 581719, FAX 336890. 2- and 7-day mountain bike tours. Camping only. Bicycles available or use your own.

- *Gametrackers (K) Ltd.* P.O. Box 62042, Nairobi, Kenya. Tel. 33892/22703. After 5:30 pm 504281. FAX 330903. 3-day mountain bike adventures. Bicycles furnished. Individualized tours arranged on request.
- *Flamboyant Bike Hire and Rides.* PO Box 69, Ukunda, Kenya. Tel. 2441 (Diani Beach), 485807 (Mombasa). 3-hour evening rides along the Coast or Shimba Hills. Special cycling safaris arranged on request.

Organized Walking Safaris
- *Yare Safaris Co. Ltd.* PO Box 63006, Nairobi, Kenya. Tel. 725610, 559313. Telex 22777. 6-day Mt. Kenya walk. 3 or more day Samburu walking safari from Maralal.
- *Executive Wilderness Programs.* c/o Let's Go Travel, Caxton House, Standard Street, PO Box 60342, Nairobi, Kenya. Tel. 340331/213033. Cable: DIKAIR. Bush-walking and mountaineering safaris: Kilimanjaro, Mt. Elgon, Mt. Suswa, Chylulu Hills, Tsavo National Park, Loita Hills.
- *Bushbuck Adventures Ltd.* PO Box 67449 (Gilfillan House, Kenyatta Ave.), Nairobi, Kenya. Tel. 60437/728737. Aberdare Mountains, Mt. Kenya and Mt. Elgon walking safaris by arrangement. For information in the UK, con-

Many of Kenya's national parks do not allow visitors outside motor vehicles for their own safety. This rhino statue is located in the Nairobi Animal Orphanage. (photo Major Aussie Walker)

tact: Wildlife Safaris, 26 Newnham Green, Maldon, Essex, CM9 6HZ. Tel. (0621) 53172.
° *Tropical Ice Ltd.* PO Box 57341, Nairobi, Kenya. Walks through Tsavo West National Park and technical climbing expeditions. For information in the United States, contact Mountain Travel-Sobek, 6420 Fairmount Ave., El Cerrito, CA. Tel. (800)227-2384, (510)527-8100.
° *Kentrak.* PO Box 47964, Nairobi, Kenya. Tel. 334112/334177. One-day walks in the Ngong Hills, 4-day treks across the Rift Valley basin.

Independent Travel

If you enjoy traveling solo, as I do, spend several hours organizing an itinerary with the help of this book. Those who travel alone inevitably meet more people. Since you will organize accommodation, food, and sightseeing, the experiences and opportunities to learn unique aspects of Kenya's social and business life will not be missed.

Asking For Directions

Any visitor who asks for directions must remember that Kenyans genuinely want to assist visitors. They do not want to say that they either do not understand the question or do not know the sought-after destination. Hence, never phrase a question by asking, "Is this the way to …?" The answer given will likely be "yes," even if they are uncertain. Instead ask, "Where does this road lead?" If they answer with the question, "Where do you want to go?" do not specify a place. Again ask where the road leads. If no direct answer is received, ask someone else.

When Kenyans are asked, "How far is it to …?" a common response is, "Not far." People are not trying to be evasive or imprecise. Time does not carry the same importance to all people. Westerners, especially, have become highly time-conscious. Many visitors discover that, after spending several weeks in Kenya, time becomes a less important consideration.

Finding a Flight (For Independent Travelers)

Fares change so rapidly that it makes little sense to quote current prices. Even as I write this, an oil crisis caused by Iraq's takeover of Kuwait has precipitated increases in transportation costs. Knowing how to find the best fare available at the time you need to travel is far more important.

Locating Bargain Fares:

☐ Visit at least three travel agencies specializing in African destinations. Secure a list of available flights and rates. Always ask:

° Are special fares available for stays of three months, 21 days, or less?

° How many stopovers does each flight make? Where? How many hours elapse between connecting flights? Some cheap fares waste too much travel time by awkward connections or long layovers.

☐ Scan the Sunday travel sections of major newspapers for discount fares. Do not assume travel agents are aware of these; often they are not. In the United States, review Sunday editions of the *Los Angeles Times* and *New York Times*. In Great Britain, scan the *Sunday Times*, *Trailfinder*, and *Time Out*.

☐ The lowest fares for US travelers to Nairobi are rarely the direct flights. First, locate a bargain fare to London, Amsterdam, or Frankfurt and then secure a second low

By spending time with the residents of rural villages, genuine friendships are developed. This Gusii mzee lives on Manga Ridge in the Kisii hills of Western Kenya.

fare between that city and Nairobi. London–Nairobi tickets can be reserved in advance but must be picked up upon arrival in London.

A reliable and efficient firm of Africa travel experts is STA Travel. In London, contact STA at 16 Bowling Green Lane, London EC1R 0BD. Tel. (071) 251-3472. In the United States, STA's New York address is 2 East 45th Street, New York, NY 10017. Tel. (212) 944-8144. STA's San Diego address is 5131 College Avenue, San Diego, CA 92115. Tel. (619) 286-1322. Call one of these offices to find another STA office closer to your home.

PanAm used to operate direct flights from New York to Nairobi, and these flights may be taken over by Delta. Air France, El Al, and British Air offer service from Los Angeles to Nairobi. British Air has a reputation for consistently dependable service on the Los Angeles–London and London–Nairobi lines. From London, Kenyan Airways and Egypt Airways offer lower fares, but with the disadvantage of several stopovers.

Measurements in Kenya

The metric system is used throughout Kenya. If you are not familiar with it, use the following conversion factors:

1 m (meter) = 3.3 feet (39 inches)
1 km (kilometer) = 0.62 mile
1 mile = 1.6 km (kilometers)
1 kg (kilogram) = 2.2 pounds
1 lb = 0.45 kg (kilogram)
1 l (liter) = 1.05 quarts
one quart = 0.95 l (liter)

CHAPTER 4

Money Matters, Customs, and Immigration

"We returned to the Makololo as poor as when we set out. Yet no distrust was shown, and my poverty did not lessen my influence (…) even my men remarked, 'Though we return as poor as we went, we have not gone in vain.'"
   David Livingstone, 1857

The Cost of Your Safari

Accommodation, meals, and transportation costs greatly determine the amount of money needed for a safari to Kenya. After securing a plane ticket and deciding whether to take an organized tour or go it alone, decide which style of travel suits your preferences and budget.

Luxury travelers (*anasa* in Swahili). Estimated cost per person: US $110, UK £70, per day.
° Stay exclusively in major tourist lodges;
° Eat only at first-class restaurants;

Fruits and vegetables, freshly picked, are for sale in roadside dukas. *The selection is vast.*

The Mennonite Guest House with its beautiful gardens and colonial charm offers budget lodging in a Nairobi suburb.

- Hire a car with a guide or a driver.

Middle-of-the-Road travelers (*katikati ya mwendo* in Swahili): Estimated cost per person: US $40–75, UK £25–50, per day.
- Vary accommodations—some luxury lodges, some smaller inns;
- Occasionally dine at splashy tourist restaurants, but most meals are taken at the top-end of locals' eateries;
- Share a rental car with others or use the train and bus when necessary.

Budget travelers (*taarifa ya gharama* in Swahili). Estimated cost per person: US $10–25, UK £7–18, per day.
- Camp or stay in hostels and small inns;
- Eat at locals' cafés or prepare own meals;
- Exclusively use public transport when necessary.

Touring Kenya can be incredibly cheap and fun, especially if cycling and walking. The most extravagant entertainment — watching a herd of leaping gazelle, a lingering gaze across the Great Rift Valley, or an afternoon walk with pastoral tribesmen — is free.

Currency

Shillings and cents are the local units of currency. One shilling or 'bob' is divided into 100 cents. In mid-1991 the rate of exchange was US $1 = 28 KS, UK £1 = 45 KS.

Money from Home

Carry only limited quantities of cash. If lost, it is not retrievable. Use travelers checks instead. *American Express* are the most widely accepted. The *Express Kenya* office is located on Standard Street near the old post office and *Let's Go Travel*. Barclays Bank appears to have more branches throughout Kenya than any other bank. Hence Barclays travelers checks should be accepted most places.

Take major credit cards. The recent introduction of a Barclay Card in Kenya has also broadened the acceptance of other major credit cards, such as Visa and MasterCard, or debit cards, mainly American Express. Even so, only the more expensive shops, hotels, and restaurants cater to cardholders.

Larger banks now accept major international cards for cash advances. If money is running out, present a major credit card to Barclays or any large bank for instant cash access. The

Locals are helpful, friendly, and patient toward foreign visitors. Time spent greeting others is highly appreciated.

currency given is Kenya shillings unless you can produce a good reason for needing foreign currency.

When exchanging traveler's checks or cash for Kenya shillings, do not accept 500 shilling notes exclusively. Insist upon 100 and 200 shilling notes which are easier to use when shopping. In rural areas the change for large notes is rarely available, so stock up on small notes of 10 and 20 shilling denominations.

Banking Hours

Most banks open from 9:00 am – 12:30 pm or 1:00 pm during weekdays. Barclays Banks in larger cities are also open Saturdays, 9:00 am – 12:00 noon.

Personal Checks

Definitely bring some personal checks. It may sound ridiculous that a stranger 12,000 miles from home might take a personal check when, in the US, a neighborhood grocer no longer will. My personal checks on a US account have been accepted on several occasions when credit cards were not honored. Bring a few, and ask to use them if the need should arise.

Black Market

Avoid exchanging money illegally. In Kenya the black market rate for the past two years has been only 15–20% above the legal rate. The risks far outweigh the benefits. If changing money illegally is still a temptation, consider this question before succumbing: Does the prospect of sleeping on a concrete floor in an unsanitary prison cell for months or years while awaiting trial appeal to you?

Be aware that there are informants who set people up, plainclothes police, and others who might have a grudge against your nationality or personality. Think of other ways to economize and make up the 20% difference.

Getting Cash at the Airport

Cash is sometimes available at the International Airports in Nairobi and Mombasa—when the banks are open and when they happen to have cash. Airport taxi drivers will probably accept dollars or pounds for the fare into the city. Local buses that service these airports will demand shillings. Before boarding these buses, ask a porter or taxi driver to exchange a few dollars or pounds at the legal rate if the banks cannot be of help.

Departure Tax

Keep US $20, or UK £15, cash for the Airport Departure Tax collected when flying out of Kenya. Travelers checks are not accepted, nor are Kenya shillings. Countless times I have overheard the desperate voices of vacationers attempting to leave the Nairobi or Mombasa Airports complaining, "My travel agent did not tell me about this."

Arrival Procedures: Customs and Immigration

Most foreign travelers arrive at Jomo Kenyatta International Airport in Nairobi. Upon departing the aircraft, you will be shown to Immigration and asked to fill out an arrival card. Hand the completed card and passport stamped with a valid Kenya visa to the first available officer. Health officials may check your International Vaccination Certificate, though this has not occurred recently.

Bicycle parts are not always available in Kenya. Jua kali *workers handcraft parts and perform repairs inexpensively.*

31

Next, proceed to the luggage area and collect all baggage. Fill out a Currency Declaration Form found on the tables in front of the Customs Officials. Present the completed form to an official with all luggage. A cursory or thorough inspection of all baggage, including your handbag, may be undertaken. The choice is theirs. Be patient and cool. (See *Getting Along with the Locals*, Chapter 8, for more hints.) If you have brought a bicycle in a carton, officials will either open the carton or ask what it contains. Assure them it is a used bicycle that you personally plan to ride, and that you will export it upon departure. If officials seem skeptical, suggest that this be written in your passport. Once Customs is cleared, you are free to leave the airport. Kenya Airways operates a bus to the city center during daylight hours for about 60 KS. To wait for the city bus, exit the terminal and walk left to the bus stop. If it is nighttime, share a taxi or wait until 6:30 am when bus service starts. Sharing a taxi with three other passengers makes the individual fare about 70 KS (US $3, UK £2).

CHAPTER 5

Equipment

"Mine was not a full-grown bicycle, but only a colt — a fifty inch, with the pedals shortened up to forty-eight — and skittish, like any other colt. The Expert explained the thing's points briefly, then he got on its back and rode around a little, to show me how easy it was to do (...) It took time to learn to miss a dog, but I achieved even that. (...) Get a bicycle. You will not regret it if you live."

Mark Twain, <u>What is Man?</u> 1906

Bicycle Recommendations

Mountain bikes, with their wide tires and sturdy frame, are ideal for touring in Kenya. Drop-handlebar ten-speeds with narrow high-pressure tires suffer more punctures and provide less stability. Some of the scenic loops suggested in this book require riding on unpaved surfaces. These graded dirt roads are not necessarily rough roads. In fact, many provide excellent surfaces for smooth cycling. However, because gravel and rock surfaces cannot be avoided entirely, a mountain bike is the recommended choice.

Outdoor shop for bicycle spares in Kericho Market, Western Kenya.

The Grand Tours and Scenic Loops described in this book are all on-road, not off-road courses. If off-road mountain cycling is your forte, deviations from the suggested routes at many points are possible. Intrepid athletes even cycle to Point Lenana atop 5,100 m (17,000 ft.) high Mt. Kenya. Now that is an off-road challenge.

A 15- to 21-speed bicycle allows anyone to conquer hills successfully and to slow down gracefully. To cycle the Easy rides, you can get by comfortably on a 1- or 3-speed bicycle. My personal preference is an 18-speed model equipped with a Spenco padded seat. If you are not a 'masochist on wheels,' join my persuasion.

Bicycle Parts

If you plan to undertake one or more of the Grand Tours the following equipment may be helpful:
- Equip tires with liners and thorn-resistant tubes.
- Attach a durable rack to the rear of the bicycle.
- Afix two or more holders for water containers.
- Mount an air pump onto the frame.
- Place bright reflectors on the front and rear of the bicycle.

Must I Take My Own Bicycle?

Three choices exist for bicycle touring in Kenya:
- Take your own bicycle;
- Purchase a bicycle in Kenya; or
- Rent a bicycle in Kenya (possible at the coast, but not in Nairobi).

Each of these options has advantages and disadvantages. You and your own bicycle are friends: you know one another and work together well. Your own bicycle likely fits your body dimensions more perfectly than any rented model. This makes for comfortable riding. It is also likely that you have learned how to perform some repairs and can troubleshoot problems quickly on a bicycle that you know well. For these reasons, bringing your own bicycle is the optimum choice. Some international airlines assess extra charges for shipping bicycles, though others count them as one of the two allowable pieces of luggage. Check with the airline company you plan to use. (See the section *Shipping Your Bicycle* in Chapter 6, *Packing Efficiently*.)

Purchasing a bicycle in Nairobi, Mombasa, Nakuru, Thika, or Kisumu may better complement your travel plans. Anyone who is not returning home directly from Kenya and who does not anticipate cycling at future destinations can purchase a bicycle in Kenya. When the cycling safari is completed, selling the bicycle for somewhat less than it cost should not be difficult.

Until recently, the only bicycles sold in Kenya were either the heavy *mambas*, used by locals as workhorses for carrying substantial loads, or lighter Taiwanese bicycles with 3 to 10 speeds. Quality English mountain bikes and English racing bicycles are now available in Nairobi. Do not expect any bicycle purchased in Kenya to be as high-performance as the custom-made one back home. Nevertheless, bicycles suitable for touring can be purchased in Kenya. Some of the best models are available at the following shops.

Shops Selling Bicycles

◦ *Inder Lakhmidar*. Nairobi. Tom Mboya Street, next to the post office. Tel. 23955. Mountain bikes: English 15 speeds, 16,500 KS; Taiwanese 12-speeds, 7,500 KS. Racing and drop-handlebar touring bicycles: English 10- or 12-

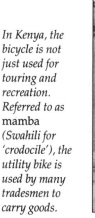

In Kenya, the bicycle is not just used for touring and recreation. Referred to as mamba *(Swahili for 'crodocile'), the utility bike is used by many tradesmen to carry goods.*

speeds, 7,800–2,000 KS; Taiwanese 10 or 12-speeds, 5,500 KS.

° *Kenya Cycle Mart Ltd*. Nairobi. Moi Avenue, Box 40787. Tel. 23417/26636. English 3-, 6-, 10- or 12-speeds, 8,500-17,000 KS.

° *Cycle Mart And Exchange*. Nairobi. Tubman Road, Box 41565. Tel. 23459/23597. Chinese heavyweight or lightweight, single speed, 2,600–2,750 KS.

Bicycle Rental

Renting a bicycle is an excellent choice for those planning to do limited cycling. At Kenya's Coast several shops rent bicycles by the day or week. Malindi, Bamburi, and Kilifi all have bicycle-hire outlets on the North Coast, as does Diani Beach Shopping Centre on the South Coast.

Bicycle Rental Stores

° *Flamboyant Bike Hire And Rides*. Diani Beach Shopping Centre. Tel. 2441; North Coast, Birges Shopping Centre, Bamburi. Tel. 485807. PO Box 69, Ukunda. Standard bicycles 750 KS per week. Mountain bikes 2,500 KS per week.

° *Sports Centre*. Diani Beach Shopping Centre. Single-speed bicycles 80 KS per day, 480 KS per week. 100 KS deposit.

° *Silver Sands Campground*. Malindi. Single-speed bicycles rented by the hour/day/week.

Do not be misled by the Pedo Company Byke Safaris and Rentals signs along the Mombasa/Malindi Highway. This company offers motorcycles only.

When Having a Bicycle is Unnecessary

Organized bicycle tours, in Nairobi, Mombasa, and Paradise Bicycle Tours in the United States, furnish bicycles, helmets, gloves, and support vehicles. (See the section *Organized Bicycle Safaris* in Chapter 3, *Pre-Trip Planning*.)

Bicycle Accessories Checklist

Whether renting, buying, or riding your own bicycle, certain cycling accessories must be brought from abroad. These items are rarely available in Kenya.

- ° Cycling helmet and gloves
- ° Handlebar bag with mapholder
- ° Panniers (if touring extensively)
- ° Water bottles and holders
- ° Detachable bicycle light
- ° Reflective tape
- ° Tire pump
- ° Patch kit

If you use your own bicycle, add:
- ° Spare tubes, spokes, and tire
- ° Basic tool kit
- ° Spare brake and derailleur cables
- ° Other essential tools and spares

Patch kits are sold in Nairobi hardware stores, but supplies of imported products are sometimes out-of-stock for months.

Ask an askari *to guard your bicycle in larger cities such as Nairobi, Mombasa, Nakuru, and Kisumu.*

Bicycle Repairs

Repairs and replacement of broken parts are amazingly simple in Kenya though few imported spares are available. Throughout the country, skillful *fundis* (Swahili for 'workers') and *jua kali* mechanics (meaning 'hot sun mechanics,' i.e. those who work outdoors) handcraft parts and perform repairs inexpensively.

The feats performed by these *jua kali* workers with limited tools and facilities is nothing short of incredible as one of my American friends recently discovered. After unpacking his bicycle in Nairobi, he found that a wheel part had been sheared into two pieces. He despaired of being able to use the bicycle because he knew such a specialized part was unobtainable in Kenya. The next day I saw him happily riding the bicycle. A capable *jua kali* worker had manufactured a usable part within a few hours.

Protecting Your Equipment

Tourists are looked upon as easy targets by unscrupulous types the world over. People on vacation are more relaxed and frequently more careless with their possessions. When leaving your bicycle anywhere, take these precautionary steps:

° Secure the bicycle with a heavy-duty chain and lock.
° In addition to the above, ask an *askari* (Swahili for 'watchman') to guard your bicycle in larger cities. Assure him that he will be paid on your return, but do not negotiate a price. Depending upon the length of your absence, tip 10–20 shillings after checking that all equipment is intact.
° In small villages where *askaris* may not be available, ask the Chief or Assistant Chief to keep the equipment during your absence. Alternately, ask a shopkeeper or one of his trusted employees to watch your possessions. At the national park gates, ask to store your gear with the Warden or Assistant Warden.
° If you have to leave equipment for several days, request an itemized receipt signed by two persons in supervisory positions. Keep the receipt with you.

CHAPTER 6

Packing Efficiently

"I had always found that the most successful travel strategy consisted in taking as few 'impedimenta' as possible and not forgetting to carry my wits about me."
    David Livingston, 1857

Everyone knows that packing lightly is important, yet most people usually lug along far more than they use. Perhaps you are uncertain about what you actually need and what items are available to purchase at your destination. This chapter will explain what you will need in Kenya.

Clothing

A few basic outfits are really all that is needed for touring Kenya. Leave highly formal clothing at home. If you enjoy the outdoors, several comfortable changes of cycling and walking attire will suffice.

Children visiting the Animal Orphanage were as curious about the author's bicycle as about the animals living there. (photo Major Aussie Walker)

Go Native

Buying local clothing is inexpensive and practical. Fashionable T-shirts sporting slogans like 'Save the Elephant' or 'Adventure on the Wild Side' are sold in many shops. Tourists soon discover the convenience of wearing the popular *kangas* (for women) and *kikois* (for men). Both are colorful rectangular pieces of cloth, about 4 feet by 6 feet in size, which are wrapped about the waist for men and women, or about the chest or neck for women only.

While Swahili men living along the coast prefer *kikois* more than slacks, local women wear their *kangas* with the greatest sense of style. A book entitled *Kangas: 101 Uses* is available. The cost for these cotton wraps is only 60–100 shillings. Besides wearing them, they are very useful as tablecloths when picnicking and groundcloths when napping.

Modesty Prevails in Kenya

"Yes, 'Knickers' are the proper dress.
Wherewith a Cycle's seat to press;
Convenient, and — should you be thrown —
Making less re-ve-la-ti-on."
    Punch, 29 September 1894

Consideration for the society in which one is a guest is the chief reason for dressing modestly. Visitors who are tolerant of the host country's standards of decency, rather than imposing their personal standards upon their hosts, find acceptance and respect. Though scantily-clad, even barebreasted women are seen in remote areas, most Kenyan men and especially women are neat and modest in their attire. Nairobi is a city where working people are dress-conscious, the men wearing suits and the women conservative dresses. When tourists choose to walk through Nairobi streets in shorts, skimpy clothing, or skin-tight cycling pants, they are tolerated but thought to be out of place by the locals.

Casual though modest dress in the rural communities is acceptable. At the beach, revealing clothes are more frequently worn by foreigners than locals. Most beaches are posted 'no topless bathing,' and it is understood that nudity is discouraged. Women are rarely seen in slacks or mini-skirts. If such restrictions seem unduly prudish, remember that Kenya is a country greatly influenced by Muslim and conservative Christian attitudes.

Easy Solutions

☐ **For Men:** Carrying a pair of slacks and a tidy shirt that can be worn over cycling clothes is a simple solution.

☐ **For Women:** A loose-fitting skirt, blouse, or simple dress provide acceptable clothing for any locality in Kenya.

☐ Choose wrinkle-resistant fabrics and colors that disguise soiled spots.

Sewing Clothes and Equipment

When clothes, bags, panniers, tents, and any cloth or leather items need repairs, capable seamstresses are available practically everywhere. In small shops and often outdoors, men and women pedal away at their sewing machines. Repairs are extremely cheap and completed on the spot. These fundis can also make new clothing or bags to your specifications. First, purchase the material, zippers, and buttons required, then locate a seamstress, and negotiate the price for tailoring.

In Nairobi, the popular streets to buy fabrics are Biashara, near the City Market, and Ngara Road, near the Globe Roundabout, where the prices are cheaper. Do not bother about locating patterns. They are unnecessary and rarely used by these skillful seamstresses.

Checklist for Clothing and Personal Items

Layering clothes is important as body temperatures fluctuate greatly when cycling and walking. Organize a simple wardrobe that allows shirts, sweaters, skirts, or slacks to be quickly pulled on or off.

- Cycling shorts, helmet, gloves
- Lightweight jacket and pants (Goretex is a recommended fabric choice)
- 2 or 3 old T-shirts (to be used eventually for bartering)
- 1 cotton long-sleeve turtleneck/pullover
- 1 skirt or pair of slacks (wrinkle-resistant)
- 2 or 3 changes of undergarments
- 1 lightweight rain parka
- 1 pair of shoes suitable for walking and cycling

- 1 pair of thongs or sandals
- 2 pairs of socks
- 1 lightweight rucksack (for walking)
- First Aid Kit & medicines you normally require
- Toiletries Kit
- Sun protection cream
- Water purifying tablets
- Optional (needed if climbing Mt. Kenya):
- 1 pair wool gloves
- 1 pair wool socks
- Lightweight underwear set (silk compresses well)
- 1 wool sweater (to be worn with Goretex jacket)

If you travel with others, the next four items can be shared among the entire party:
- Binoculars (powerful, lightweight model such as the Nikon Companion Venturer II)
- Camera with zoom lens and film
- Swiss Army Knife (model with scissors, screwdriver, bottle and can opener)
- Small sewing kit

Chai Supplies

Chai (which literally means 'tea') are small items given to someone either to express gratitude for help or to garner favors from those whose help is desired. They help smooth over many delicate situations. The *Chai* supplies suggested on the following list are inexpensive and lightweight. Stow them in a bag until an appropriate situation arises. Many of these items are available in Kenya, but those brought from abroad are especially valued.
- Postcards or photos of your homeland
- Bandannas
- T-shirts (advertising your home state or country)
- Baseball or cycling caps
- Inexpensive wristwatches, earrings, rings
- Attractive pen and pencil sets
- Small mirrors or combs
- Small boxes of matches or cigarette lighters
- Cigarettes (to be given away one at a time)
- Pocket knives
- Candies, locally referred to as sweets
- Small soap bars, toothbrushes, and toothpaste

You can let someone else do the planning for you. Participants in an organized luxury bicycle safari line up before the start.

- Rubber thongs and plastic sandals costing about 20 shillings are highly appreciated in rural areas. Both are bulkier than the other items. If space allows, tuck a medium-size pair or two into your bags.

Camping Gear

"I was given a tent, much to my satisfaction, for there was nothing I liked better than tents. By day their hot, jungly smell, as thick as treacle, was delightful, and the dark-green gloom inside reminded me of Turkish delight. At night they had the atavistic charm of caves: a warm, protecting, secret cave, a refuge, and a private kingdom."

    Elspeth Huxley, <u>The Flame Trees of Thika</u>, 1959

Budget travelers and those who revel in nights spent sleeping under the stars should bring a minimal camping kit to Kenya. Many villages, even remote ones, have small lodges or *bandas* (Swahili for 'basic shelters'). Rural people are often generous and will share their homes as well. Some visitors find staying in locals' homes a unique experience; others object to the standards of cleanliness or simply prefer their privacy. Nevertheless, camping is usually a preference rather than a necessity. It is only when hiking into the mountains or far back into the bush that a tent becomes a necessary shelter. Mt. Kenya and Mt. Elgon, Kenya's two highest mountains, both offer huts.

Carrying a small tent and sleeping bag provide the flexibility to stay anywhere. If this option interests you, the checklist below delineates what is available in Kenya and what must be brought from abroad.

Camping Gear Checklist

These items must be purchased abroad, since they are not readily available locally.
- Lightweight tent
- Tent seam sealant (1 small tube)
- Lightweight sleeping bag
- Therma-Rest Mattress or foam mat
- Two cooking pots (locally called *surfurias*)
- Mug
- Fork and spoon (if not included with Swiss Army Knife)
- Matches
- Flashlight and extra batteries

Fuel for modern lightweight campstoves may not be available in Kenya unless they burn kerosene or gasoline. No white gas or butane canisters are sold. Bluet or Camping Gaz canisters cost about 45 shillings and are sold in hardware stores in Nairobi when supplies are available. Locals use wood or charcoal fires for outdoor cooking. Somehow they make soaked timber burst into flame. You will create blazing fires by following their techniques.

Supplies Can Be Exhausted

Do not become frustrated when items easily purchased back home cannot be found. This is not home; this is Kenya, a relatively undeveloped country where most goods are imported. Put simply, this means that when the ship does not deliver, store shelves remain empty. During the years I have lived in Kenya, shortages of flour, lightbulbs, nails, sugar, and cooked cereal have existed.

Reading Material

Travelers on the move must minimize weight without forfeiting the benefits of necessary reading material. Despite the extensive research undertaken in preparation for your safari, avoid loading bags with heavy books by following the following hints.

☐ Photocopy the pages of books that will be most helpful during the safari.

☐ Cut down further on weight when photocopying material by (a) requesting reductions (unless your eyesight will not tolerate small print), (b) insisting that copies be made on the front and back of individual pages, and (c) trimming all excess edges from these finished sheets.

☐ Practice the concept of sharing. If journeying with other amateur ornithologists or botanists, divide the necessary books among participants, avoiding the burden of duplication.

Shipping Your Bicycle

Transporting a bicycle by air presents few problems. Check with the airline about baggage weight restrictions. A bicycle rarely weighs more than 45 pounds (20 kg). Small, heavy, items

If you choose a moderate approach to active touring, select specific areas to cycle or walk, and use public transportation or a hired car to get to your next destination. (photo Major Aussie Walker)

can be packed in one bag and carried on the plane as cabin luggage.

Ask the airline if any special packing requirements exist for bicycles. Though opinions vary on how to ship a bicycle, three methods are commonly used:

◦ Obtain a cardboard carton from the airline, a bicycle shop, or Amtrak. Remove the pedals and turn the handlebars before placing the bicycle into the carton.

◦ Purchase a soft bicycle travel bag. This option necessitates partial disassembly of the bicycle.

◦ Roll the bicycle onto the plane as it is.

Packing Panniers Efficiently

Daytrippers can manage with a handlebar bag or a small waistpack while cycling. Those undertaking tours of several days or longer without motor vehicle support need a bicycle rack and at least two panniers. Because panniers are rarely waterproof, clothing and supplies must be packed in heavy plastic bags. Balance the load left and right, placing heavy items on the bottom. Develop an order for loading the panniers, putting certain items in the same location everyday. Anything needed frequently while riding (such as a camera, binoculars, toilet paper, or tools) should go into the most easily accessible pockets.

CHAPTER 7

Health, Water, Food, and Sex

"Eating should always be an affair of pleasure. If food be the music of love then the visitor to Nairobi is going to find love at every street corner. The variety of restaurants is kaleidoscopic."
  Kate Macintyre, The Nairobi Guide, 1986

Health Services Available

Health services abound in Kenya. Nairobi boasts two large hospitals, the Nairobi and Aga Khan, and many private clinics. Pharmacies (called 'chemists') are numerous and well-stocked in the larger cities. There is even the Flying Doctors Service, a small fleet of doctor-pilots who respond to emergency calls by air.

Finding dentists or ordering new eyeglasses is no problem in Nairobi or Mombasa. Eyeglasses are made within one or two days at reasonable prices. Eye-testing is also available if a prescription is necessary. Competent dental work, including new crowns for teeth, is readily available and inexpensive.

Nairobi's City Hall was built after Kenya's Independence in 1963.

The following healthcare facilities are ones I have personally used and can recommend:

° *Seventh Day Adventist Health Services.* Milimani Road, Nairobi. Tel. 721200/1. Services: General Practitioner, Ob/gyn, Dentist, Immunizations for hepatitis, etc.
° *Dr. Devani.* Bruce House, Standard Street, Nairobi. Tel. 29091/331833. Services: Dentist (Several dental offices are located in Bruce House and Nairobi Hospital).
° *Optica.* Moi Avenue, Box 41625, Nairobi. Tel. 20516/ 336754. Services: Eye testing. One-day service for new glasses. Large frame selection.
° *Lens Ltd.* Kenyatta Avenue, Box 49608, Nairobi. Tel. 23556. Services: Eye testing. One or two day service for new glasses.
° *Monk's, The Chemist.* Kimathi Street near the New Stanley, Nairobi. Tel. 22702. Hours: 9:00 am – 6:30 pm Monday–Friday, 9:00 am – 2:30 pm Saturday.
° *KAM Pharmacy.* Kimathi Street near the New Stanley, Nairobi. Tel. 722834/29137. Hours: 8:00 am – 6:00 pm Monday–Friday, 8:00 am – 1:30 pm Saturday.

Antimalarials

"Malaria is preventable. You need not catch malaria if you are sensible."
Dr. A. Turner, The Traveller's Health Guide

Start taking antimalarials two weeks prior to travel. Many British physicians prescribe a daily dose of Paludrine and a once/weekly dose of Daraprim or Maloprim. American authorities recommend Chloroquine taken once/weekly.

For additional protection, wear long trousers and long-sleeved shirts after dusk. Spray exposed skin with an insect repellent. Several brands are available at supermarkets and chemists throughout Kenya.

Mosquitoes are not a concern at higher altitudes, but the coastal lowlands and Lake Victoria vicinity are malarial. In these areas use mosquito-proof netting over the bed and keep windows shut at night.

Mosquito coils are inexpensive and effective. Purchase them at supermarkets and chemists. Antimalarial tablets require no prescription and cost little in Kenya — about 100 shillings (US $5.00, UK £3) for a two-month supply. When planning a long visit, save money by purchasing only the dosage needed prior to arrival. Then stock up in Nairobi at a fraction of the price you would pay abroad.

If these sensible precautions are followed, the chances of contracting malaria are greatly diminished. Further reading about this disease is available in *The Travellers' Health Guide* by Anthony C. Turner, Roger Lascelles Publishers, London.

AIDS, Etcetera

AIDS is a killer. There is scarcely a country in the world where the AIDS virus does not exist. Risking infection through casual sex is unnecessary. Condoms can be purchased at chemists' shops in Kenya's larger cities. Contraceptive gels, however, are nonexistent. Bring these products from abroad.

Drinking Water

Most visitors are rightfully concerned about the safety of drinking water during their stay. While Nairobi's water supply is generally considered safe, the water supplies in other cities are questionable.

When traveling outside Nairobi, take the precaution of drinking soda water, mineral water, soft drinks, or beer. All are inexpensive and widely available. Soft drinks (called sodas) cost only four shillings and large beers (*pombe kubwa* in Swahili) are 15 shillings.

Recycling bottles is a necessity observed rigorously throughout Kenya. Many shops, in smaller villages particularly, do not allow bottles to be purchased. Sodas or beers must be imbibed on the premises. Undoubtedly, thirsty cyclists and walkers will want to stow several bottles in their packs. The solution is to buy a few bottles the first chance you get and carry these bottles to trade for the next drinks you purchase. By trading used bottles, you are always free to take away new bottled drinks. Bottled mineral water used to be expensive because it was imported — but no more. Since Robert Link founded Kilimanjaro Mineral Waters Limited, a delicious and reasonably-priced product is available.

Sterilizing Water

With inexpensive bottled drinks available, it is unlikely that you will need to sterilize water often. Choose one of these three methods to make water safe for drinking when necessary.

☐ Boiling. Keep water boiling for at least two minutes — one minute longer for every 1,000 feet above sea level.

☐ Filtering. Purchase lightweight portable filters from abroad. They are unavailable in Kenya. A simpler solution is to carry a piece of finely woven fabric through which the water is poured. If fine, clean sand is available, a sand filter is easily improvised by using a sock or tin can with a hole in the bottom. Pour the water over the sand and collect the water that drains through.

☐ Purifying tablets. Such tablets are usually iodine based, fast acting, and effective. Iodine produces physiological side effects, however, and should not be used over an extended time.

Food

"… we all live on dead animals, like hyenas and lions. I used to think that vegetarians were cranks, but now I wonder; perhaps they have climbed a rung higher on the ladder of civilization. Perhaps it is more spiritual to live on beans and spinach, with possibly an egg now and then."
Elspeth Huxley, *The Flame Trees of Thika*, 1959

Vegetables and fruits, usually freshly picked from the garden, are for sale in the stores called greengrocers and roadside *dukas* (Swahili for 'small shops'). Vegetarians will think they have died-and-gone-to-heaven, for the selection is vast. These basics are widely available: cabbage, lettuce, carrots, tomatoes, cucumbers, peppers, okra, coconuts, bananas, papayas, oranges, and greens. The latter is a staple of the working-class diet and is called *sukuma wiki,* meaning literally 'to push on the week,' which this cheap food presumably helps many to do.

Try to sample exotic fruits like tomato fruits, passion fruits, custard apples, guava, and mangoes. Roasted ears of corn are popular streetside snacks, served without salt or butter. These roasted ears are addictive, as many discover after developing a taste for them.

Tilapia and Nile perch are the most common fish. Many are taken from Lake Turkana by Luos, a Western Kenya tribe, who migrated north to develop a profitable fishing trade. Although the Samburu people live in the Lake Turkana region, they, like the Masai, are not fisheaters. Many Africans like meat. That is why *nyama choma* (roasted beef) cafés are numerous. Beef, pork, lamb, and goat are popular choices. Tourists in search of unusual meats like zebra, gazelle, or crocodile must visit Nairobi's Carnivore Restaurant.

Hoteli, sometimes shortened to 'hotel,' generally means a small café, not a place of lodging. Restaurant, cafeteria, and snack bar also designate establishments offering food. Dining out in Nairobi and Mombasa costs surprisingly little — about 100 shillings per person — unless meals are taken at places catering to tourists, where prices are substantially higher. Some restaurant recommendations:

Indian:
° The Minar (Nairobi. three locations — Sarit Centre, Tel. 748359; Yaya Centre, Tel. 561676, and Banda Street, Tel. 29999)

Chinese:
° Hong Kong (Nairobi. Koinange Street, Tel. 28612; Mombasa. Moi Avenue, Tel. 26707)
° Rickshaw. (Nairobi. Fedha Towers, Tel. 23604)

Italian:
° Marino's (Nairobi. National Housing Corporation Building, Aga Khan Walkway, opposite the American Cultural Centre, Tel. 27150/337230)

French:
° Alan Bobbe's Bistro (Nairobi. Caltex House, Koinange Street, Tel. 26027)
° Jardin De Paris (Nairobi. French Cultural Centre, Loita Street, Tel. 336435)

Steaks:
° The Horseman (Karen. Karen Shopping Centre, Tel. 882033/882782)
° The Red Bull (Nairobi. Silopak House, Mama Ngina Street, Tel. 335717/28045)
° The Carnivore (Nairobi. Langata Rd., Tel. 501799)

Pizza:
° The Pizza Garden at The Horseman (See *Steaks*)
° The Pizza Garden (Nairobi, Jacaranda Hotel, Westlands Suburb)
° The Pizzeria (Malindi, coastal road)

Elegant Dining:
- Tamarind (Mombasa. Cross Nyali Bridge from Mombasa, turn right; Nairobi. Harambee Avenue, opposite the American Cultural Centre, Tel. 20473)
- Kentmere Club (9 miles, 15 km, west of Nairobi on Old Limuru Rd.)

Outdoor Dining:
- Toona Tree (Nairobi, International Casino, Museum Hill)
- Gringo's (3 miles, 5 km, west of Nairobi on C62)

Most Nostalgic:
- Delamere Bar and Grill (Nairobi, Norfolk Hotel, Tel. 335422)

Best Burgers:
- Burger Hut (Nairobi, Apic Centre, Westlands)
- The Harvest (Nairobi, Kenyatta Avenue, vegetarian only)

Light Lunches:
- JAX Restaurant (Nairobi. Old Mutual Building, 1st Floor, Kimathi Street, Tel. 28365/29145)
- SANA Cafeteria (Nairobi, Wabera Street)
- Hurlingham Hotel (Nairobi, Argwings Kodhek Road)
- Sugar & Spice (Nairobi, Yaya Centre, 2nd Floor)
- La Belle Inn (Naivasha, town centre)

Most Filling Lunches:
- The Supreme and Mayur Indian Restaurants (Nairobi, Kilome Road, off Tom Mboya Street)

Best Afternoon Tea:
- Elsamere (Naivasha, South Moi Lake Road, Joy Adamson's former home)

Ice Cream:
- Nairobi Suburbs: Sarit Centre, Yaya Centre, Apic Centre
- Nairobi City Centre: Koinange Street

Milkshakes:
- Burger Hut (See *Best Burgers*)

Best Local Beers:
- Tusker (regular, export, and supreme)
- White Cap (regular, export)

Best Local Wine:
- Lake Naivasha white or red.

CHAPTER 8

Getting Along with the Locals

"I speak to them and treat them as rational beings, and generally get on well with them in consequence."
  David Livingstone, 1857

Meeting the Kenyan people is one of the most delightful features of any safari to this country. In general, locals are friendly, helpful, and patient towards foreign guests. Their smiles are broad, and their hospitality is equally expansive. Most have not let their lives become so frantic that they under-value the importance of time spent greeting others. Harried western travelers can learn much from observing how Kenyans interact and the priority these meetings take in their daily routine.

  A cycling and walking tour provides the ideal conditions for meeting the indigenous people. Countless times I have been the recipient of food, shelter, assistance, and gifts. Recently a man whose clothes were literally in shreads offered me the correct coins to use a pay telephone. When I tried to repay him with a larger coin, he refused the money saying, "Anyone can help." While walking in the Cherangani Hills for several

Kamba children on Kiima-Kilwe, the sacred hill above Machakos (see Western Kenya Loop 1, chapter 15).

weeks, I was offered shelter and dinner every night and given decorated milk gourds. This hospitality was extended by Pokots, one of Kenya's most unacculturated and aloof tribes.

Dispelling the Myths

Unfortunately, many tourists arrive in Kenya with negative preconceptions about the people: "They are beggars." "Watch out for your purse." "Don't trust any of them." Such ideas, quite naturally, make visitors wary. The safaris they join are organized in a style that isolates them from most residents, so they leave Kenya having met only the locals who work in the tourist industry.

By relaxing and spending time with residents, especially in the mountains and rural villages, you may develop friendships which are not predicated upon the amount of money you carry. A few hints about getting along with the locals may smooth the way to a troublefree vacation.

Protocol: Meeting the Chief

When staying overnight in smaller villages, it is considered good manners to greet the Chief. He (I have met no women chiefs) is a leader elected by the residents, whose job is to oversee the welfare of the people. Before setting up camp, ask anyone where to find the Chief's home (in the absence of the Chief, ask for the Assistant Chief). Then go to his home and request permission to stay in the village. Once there, inquire about where the most secure and convenient place to camp might be. This gesture will give you, the guest, additional security. When the Chief knows of your presence, he alerts others of his desire for your safety.

Presenting a small gift to the Chief is not obligatory, but it is considered good manners. After all, you are asking for a favor (to camp safely in his community). Giving a small token of friendship in return is reasonable. This is when the *Chai* Supplies come in handy.

Many Chiefs do not fit the fictionalized image of a Chief at all. Instead of feather head-dresses and painted chests, most Chiefs these days wear sports jackets, slacks, and ties. The desire to emulate western fashion is powerful.

Using Guides

People who live in rural areas have had few opportunities for contact with foreigners. Understandably, they may be suspicious about the motives of strangers who visit. Using local guides when walking in remote areas is highly recommended for several reasons:

☐ A guide may know the best trails to reach villages, mountaintops, or wherever. While trailfinding on your own, it is possible to wander inadvertently into areas where the presence of strangers is unappreciated. For example, in the hills above Machakos, there are certain rocks and forests considered sacred to the Akamba. Nothing, not even a tree branch, should be removed from these places.

☐ A guide is an excellent source of information about his or her people, their customs, and history. Walking with locals provides access to firsthand knowledge of unique tribal traditions.

☐ A guide provides security. Other tribesmen are relaxed about the presence of visitors accompanied by a local friend. In fact, the guide's relatives will probably invite you into their homes. Such relaxed times spent visiting together provide the best opportunities for understanding another culture.

No horse trading here: just a little camel dealing, as the author's bicycle changes hands for a camel. The deal did not pan out, because the camel refused to go along with its new owner. (photo Major Aussie Walker)

☐ By employing a guide, you help a local family. Be generous and fair in payments. When in doubt about what
amount to pay, it is better to err on the side of over-gene-
rosity than to learn later you acted niggardly.

Police Checks and Patience

Do not be intimidated by police or military checkpoints. These
occur frequently along the main roadways and are not as
ominous as they at first appear. Most of the time the police are
checking to see that car and insurance registrations are up-to-
date or that buses are not overloaded. Relax and follow these
suggestions:

☐ Do not attempt to circumvent a police check. You are
obliged to stop until signaled to proceed.

☐ If the police ask you any questions, or want to search
your baggage, do not become defensive. Speak slowly,
clearly, and softly. Give a specific answer if asked where
you are headed. Do not sound vague.

☐ Be patient. Behave as though you have all the time in the
world to chat with the police.

☐ Be genuinely pleasant. Smile. Let the police know you understand their need to perform checks and that you ap-
preciate their work.

☐ Never become authoritative when you need police assistance. Start your request by saying, "I wonder if you
could help me…"

By practicing these suggestions, you will whiz through police
checks without a problem 99.9% of the time.

Opinions about the Government and President

Avoid public statements about the government and its leaders
lest your intentions in visiting Kenya be misunderstood. There
is only one President in Kenya; no one else is referred to by
that title. Others in leadership positions are termed managers,
chairmen/chairwomen, provosts, commissioners, or directors
— never President. Joking publicly about the government and
its leaders should be avoided.

Transacting Business — *Hakuna Matata*

"The Kikuyu did not reckon time in years, new or old, or in any way cut it up into sections. It flowed on like a stream."
Elspeth Huxley, <u>The Flame Trees of Thika</u>, 1959

Whereas the western world is zealous about efficiency in business transactions, Kenyans are more influenced by the spirit of *hakuna matata*. The literal meaning is 'no problem,' but this expression is frequently meant to calm people who appear rushed or worried.

Inevitably tourists become frustrated while waiting in a slow-moving line at the bank or post office. Before exploding, consider the positive aspects of conducting business in a relaxed and friendly manner where people are not treated like anonymous entities. Visitors to Kenya are happier once they, too, adopt the *hakuna matata* spirit. Slowing down is healthy. Cyclists and walkers also value the slower pace which allows them to make contact with their surroundings. While waiting for service in a restaurant, why not use the extra time to explore what is happening around you? Invite several locals to have a drink. Chat with them about their jobs, homes (Kenyans identify with their place of birth as 'home'), work, and families. Service seems to progress much faster after accepting the *hakuna matata* point of view.

Photography

Always ask first before photographing anyone. Some may object because they do not understand cameras or believe the picture removes part of their souls. When I first arrived to Kenya, I tried photographing a group of tea pickers without asking for permission. Once I was spotted, everyone dropped down into the tea bushes and remained there until I left. Now I approach one person, show my camera, and ask for permission.

"Nataka kupiga picha, tafadhali" is Swahili for "I would like to take a picture, please." The answer may be *"hapana,"* or "no," in which case you should leave. If the answer is *"Nataka chai"* ("I want some payment"), you may offer a *chai* gift or small payment of 5–20 shillings. It is difficult not to be angered by anyone asking for money simply to be photographed. Try to understand that these are poor people and, in reality, a favor

is being asked. If you want to stay out of trouble, always ask before clicking the shutter.

Never photograph anything that might be considered important to national security in the broadest sense. Military installations and uniformed police or military officers are off-limits to photographers. If you ask such persons for permission to photograph them, they are under orders to refuse.

Bribes — *Chai* for Favors

"It is thus a sort of blackmail that these insignificant chiefs levy; and the native traders, in paying, do so simply as a bribe to keep them honest."
David Livingstone, 1857

Two kinds of *chai* or gift-giving exist in Kenyan society. One is something given by someone when motivated by appreciation or kindness. Nothing is expected in return. The other is a payment given with the expectation of receiving something in return. This is, in fact, a bribe.

Should bribes ever be paid? This truly depends upon your judgment about the situation. How badly do you need help? What are your chances of getting the necessary aid if a bribe is refused? Visitors to Third World Countries may dig in their cultural and moral heels, insisting that bribery is dishonest and corrupt. By refusing to pay any bribes, they hope to reform the system. Frustration and alienation are the results of such attempts to mold, rather than to meet, the locals.

If bribes are solicited in Kenya, remember that dishonesty and corruption exist in the western world as well. It is easy to wear blinders to some extent and to overlook the ways Westerners purchase privileges at times. Buying tickets from 'hawkers' is one example of paying a bribe or premium to get something desired. I am not building a case for condoning bribery anywhere. But don't be too sacrosanct in your attitude about its usage in Third World Countries.

When an official suggests that you buy him some lunch or give him *chai*, one option is to politely refuse. Another is to claim that you are out of money (which he will find hard to believe since you are traveling, which he cannot afford to do). Adopt the habit of carrying little cash — at least where it is easily visible. When opening your wallet, it should reveal 100 shillings or less. If you are not making any headway without paying a bribe, show the money that your wallet contains. Ask if some portion can be retained for your own lunch, and give the rest.

Salaries are extremely low for these people. When they see the luxuries foreigners possess, they recognize the chance to have a bit extra. Not all are greedy or out to take advantage of every tourist. Any additional money for them most likely means having meat with a meal or having school fees for a child. I try not to be a soft-touch, but I have paid some bribes and probably will pay more.

Cheating

Being cheated differs from being asked for a bribe. Do not knowingly let anyone cheat you by making the wrong change or similar actions. Although a few dishonest types give the rest a bad name, most people in Kenya are scrupulously honest. Not long ago, for example, two men ran after me in Nairobi to return eyeglasses which had fallen from my purse. "We wanted you not to be without your glasses," one of them explained. They were motivated by honest intentions and departed asking nothing for their trouble.

Language

Kiswahili or Swahili is spoken by almost everyone in Kenya though it is not a native language to Africa. Arab merchants

Those who travel alone, as the author did cycling to Vipingo, inevitably meet more people. (photo Major Aussie Walker)

who traded up and down the East African coast for over a thousand years developed the language from coastal dialects with the addition of many Arab words. Today the language is spoken in East Africa and parts of Central Africa.

For visitors to Kenya, speaking Swahili is not essential. Most locals speak at least three languages including basic English, Swahili, and a tribal dialect or 'mother tongue.' In remote areas where residents have had little contact with educated people, English may not be spoken.

Learning some basic Swahili is easy, fun, and appreciated by Kenyans who will notice your efforts to communicate in their language. Note that Swahili spellings frequently vary for the same words. For this reason you may see Swahili words spelled differently in this book. Variant spellings are common. Even the spelling for one of Kenya's largest tribes, Maasai and Masai, is inconsistent. A set of two Swahili conversation cassettes can be ordered from Educational Services, 1725 K Street, NW, Suite 408, Washington DC 20006 USA. Request the *Language/30 Educational Services Teaching Cassettes — Kiswahili*. Swahili phrasebooks can be purchased at many bookstores in Nairobi and Mombasa (see *Bookstore Recommendations*, in Chapter 11, *Getting Started in Nairobi*). A list of Swahili terms especially helpful to cyclists and walkers, designed to be photocopied and carried in a wallet, is included Appendix.

Recommended Reading

Understanding a country whose culture and history differ greatly from one's own is expedited by reading. Generally, the more that is known about a place, the easier it is to get along with the residents and to respect their customs.

History:
° *The Lunatic Express*, Charles Miller. Westlands Sundries Press, Nairobi.
  The White Nile, Alan Moorehead. Penguin Books, U K.
° *Straight On Till Morning — The Biography of Beryl Markham*, Mary S. Lovell. Hutchinson Press, London.
° *White Man's Country — Lord Delamere and the Making of Kenya*, Volume I and II, Elspeth Huxley. Chatto and Windus, London.
° *Out of Africa*, Karen Blixon (Isak Dinesen, ps.). Penguin Books, UK.
° *African Lives*, Dennis Boyles. Ballantine Books, New York.

Journey to the Jade Sea, John Hillaby. Paladin, UK.
° *The Tree Where Man Was Born,* Peter Matthiessen. Picador, UK.
West With the Night, Beryl Markham. Penguin Books, UK.
° *One Life, An Autobiography*, Richard E. Leakey. Salem House, Topsfield, Massachusetts.
° *Pokot, Meru,* (and other major tribes). Small paperback books published by the Consolata Fathers, Nairobi; distributed by Text Book Centre, Box 47540, Nairobi.

Guidebooks:
° *Spectrum Guide to Kenya,* Camerapix, editor. Westlands Sundries Ltd., Nairobi.
° *Camping Guide to Kenya*, David Else. Bradt Publications, UK.
° *Rough Guide to Kenya*, Richard Trillo. Harrap-Columbus Ltd., London. *East Africa, A Travel Survival Kit.* Geoff Crowther. Lonely Planet, Australia.
° *Backpacker's Africa, East and Southern*, Hilary Bradt. Bradt Publications (UK).
° *The Traveller's Handbook*, Melissa Shales, editor. Wexas Ltd, London.
° *The Nairobi Guide*, Kate Macintyre. Macmillan, London.

Field Guides:
° *Wayside Flowers of Kenya*, Teresa Sapieha. Published by author, Box 43096, Nairobi.
° *African Blossoms*, Dorothy and Bob Hargreaves. Hargreaves Company, Inc., Box 895, Kailua, Hawaii 96734 USA
° *Beautiful Birds of Kenya*, John Karmali. Westlands Sundries Ltd., Box 14107, Nairobi.
° *Animals of East Africa*, C.T. Astley Maberly. Stodder and Stoughton, Nairobi.
° *Field Guide to the Birds of East Africa*, J.G. Williams and Norman Arlott. Collins, London.
° *Field Guide to the Mammals of East Africa*, Theodor Haltenorth and Helmut Diller. Collins, London.
° *Field Guide to the Larger Mammals of East Africa*, Jean Dorst and Pierre Dandelot. Collins, London.

Health:
° *The Traveller's Health Guide*, Dr. Anthony C. Turner. Roger Lascelles, London.

61

Maps

A trip to the Government Map Office in Nairobi will likely prove unprofitable. Most of the Survey of Kenya Maps are no longer available. You might try presenting an official-looking letter stating why a particular map is needed, but the chances of securing maps are slim. Various maps of Kenya, Nairobi, and the National Parks can be bought in Nairobi Bookstores (See *Bookstore Recommendations*, in Chapter 11, *Getting Started in Nairobi*). These local maps often lack detail and contain inaccuracies.

The maps provided in this book should be sufficient for planning a limited or extensive safari. If larger or more elaborate maps are desired, these can be ordered from the shops listed below.

Map Outlets — USA:

Map Centre, Inc.
2611 University Avenue
San Diego, CA 92104-2894
Tel. (619) 291-3830

Hammond Map and Travel
Center
57 W. 43rd. Street
New York, NY 10036
Tel. (212) 398-1222

Wide World Bookshop
1911 N. 45th Street
Seattle, WA 98103
Tel. (206) 634-3453

Maplink
25 E. Mason St.
Santa Barbara, CA 93101
Tel. (805) 965-4402
FAX (805) 962-0884

Map Outlets — UK:

Heffers Booksellers
3rd Floor, 19 Sidney Street
Cambridge CB23HL
Tel. (0223) 358-351

McCarta Ltd.
122 King's Cross Road
London WC1X 9DS
Tel. (01) 278-8276

The Map Shop
15 High Street,
Upton-upon-Severn
Worcestershire, WR8 DHJ
Tel. (06846) 3146

CHAPTER 9

Wildlife in the Parks and Outside

"More accidents happen by the buffalo, and the black rhinoceros, than by the lion. Though all are aware of the mischievous nature of the buffalo (...) our young men went after him (...) as a buffalo charges back in a forest, [they] dart dexterously out of his way behind a tree, and, wheeling round it, stab him as he passes."
  David Livingstone, 1857

Before coming to Kenya, many foreigners have only seen wild animals in zoos. The thought of meeting such animals while walking or cycling is disconcerting to say the least. "Won't the lions eat me?" one visitor recently queried.

It is highly unlikely that you will glimpse lions or similar predatory animals outside the national parks. By nature these animals shy away from human contact. The Kalenjin of Kenya tell a folk story explaining why:

Roadblock ahead. This ostrich never bothered to look back at the approaching cyclists. Most wild animals avoid contact with people.

"The Earth and the Sky"

"Why are the sun, moon and stars up in the sky, while Man and the animals are on the earth?"

"Once the sun, moon and stars were on the earth with Man and the animals, but they became frightened and went away. You see, they once all slept together, motionless, on their sides. All except Man. One day Sun noticed him turn his head, and he grew suspicious. Soon afterwards Man turned right over. Sun, Moon and Stars were alarmed, and decided to go away into the sky to see what would happen. When they had gone, Man got up and walked away. He made himself weapons from stones, and he killed small animals for food, and larger animals to provide him with skins to cover his body. He made a boat and caught fish. The animals began to be afraid of him. Elephant, and the other big animals realized that it was too late to escape into the sky, so they hid in the forest, and they have been hiding from Man ever since."

People of the Rift Valley, Kalenjin, Benjamin Kipkorir, Evans Brothers (Kenya) Ltd., Nairobi.

Better roads and 4-wheel drive vehicles have popularized travel throughout Kenya. Today, it is only the active traveler who explores the country by bike or on foot who realizes a genuine closeness to the land and the people. (photo Major Aussie Walker)

Hundreds of species of non-threatening wild animals and birds are readily visible outside Kenya's national parks.

Wildlife Outside the Parks

Herds of nonthreatening plains animals and hundreds of varieties of birds are readily visible outside the national parks. This is one of the real treats for cyclists and walkers who see far more than tourists speeding along the highways. By taking the uncongested backroads and hiking trails, zebra, gazelle, giraffe, antelope, dikdik, duiker, baboon, monkeys, and many other animals can be quietly observed away from the 'tourist scene.'

For example, few people have ever seen the evasive Greater Kudu, a magnificent animal. Yet, while riding a bicycle near Lake Bogoria, I saw a dozen kudu and many curious dikdik who stood on the roadside watching my approach. Such are the joys of backroad travel....

Birdwatching

Over 1,300 varieties of birds inhabit Kenya in contrast to 60 different mammals. In this veritable paradise for birdwatchers, a staggering array of birds can be spotted from the tiniest colorful bee-eaters to the grey Goliath Herons standing over five feet tall. Even novice birdwatchers report distinguishing 50 different species while visiting Lake Baringo. The Rift Valley Lakes provide superb birdwatching arenas (See *Great Rift*

65

Valley Wonders, Chapter 16), as do the Kakamega Forest and Cherangani Hills (see *Northwest Kenya and the Cherangani Hills*, Chapter 18). Tourists who come to Kenya primarily to photograph the 'Big Five' mammals, frequently leave Kenya having become avid birdwatchers.

Wildlife Dangers

"One is in much more danger of being run over when walking the streets of London, than he is of being devoured by lions in Africa."
  David Livingstone, 1852

The most aggressive African animals are the elephant and the buffalo. If startled, these animals have been known to charge at people. It is unlikely that you will cycle through areas inhabited by these animals, but hiking into such places is probable. For example, the approaches to Mt. Kenya's Chogoria and Naro Moru Routes lead through bush country where elephant and buffalo roam. Walking in Aberdare National Park and the forests near Kwale in the Shimba Hills are other likely places to encounter these animals.

When entering such areas you will likely be accompanied by a guide who will hear these aggressive animals first. If, in the rare event, you find yourself alone with potentially dangerous animals, take these precautions:

☐ Make noise. Most animals who can hear or smell your approach will move away from you. A startled animal can become a dangerous animal.

☐ Stay in open spaces. Since surprised animals are more likely to attack, allow them to openly view you.

☐ Definite Don'ts:
- Don't get between a hippo and the water.
- Don't get between a mother elephant (or any other wild animal) and her baby.
- Don't swim in water where crocodiles and hippos have staked their claim.

☐ Finally, should you come upon a buffalo, look for a climbable tree. If there are none, stay calm, behave confidently, and stand still or move away very slowly.

Cycling and Walking Through National Parks.

Most of Kenya's national parks do not allow people to enter without motor vehicles because of the sheer numbers and density of potentially threatening animals. Two national parks allow cyclists and walkers, and neither should be missed.

Hell's Gate National Park near Lake Naivasha (see *Loop 2, Hell's Gate and Lake Naivasha*, in Chapter 16, *Great Rift Valley Wonders*) allows guests in cars and on bicycle and foot. This park is impressive in several ways; for its abundance of plains animals such as eland and hartebeest, and for its steaming geothermal station. Saiwa Swamp National Park near Kitale (see *Loop 2, Saiwa Swamp National Park*, in Chapter 18, *Northwest Kenya and the Cherangani Hills*) allows walkers only; cars and bicycles are left at the entrance gate. As its name suggests, the park is indeed situated in a swamp where the rare and semi-aquatic Sitatunga Antelope lives. Wooden bridges and tree-houses allow visitors access into the swamp.

Remember that Kenya's National Parks charge entrance fees. The 1990 rates for non-residents are: Adults 200 KS, Children 20 KS, Car 20 KS. Residents pay less: Adults 40 KS, Children 10 KS, Car 20 KS.

Millions of flamingos at Lake Bogoria, one of the Great Rift Valley's many soda lakes.

National Parks Requiring Motor Vehicles

To enter the remaining national parks requires a motorized vehicle. Since cyclists and walkers view an abundance of wild animals and birdlife outside the national park boundaries, they are less likely to schedule many days inside the national parks. Crowded conditions mar some parks, especially during the high season when safari vans form long dusty processions surrounding the animals.

The more adventurous side of Kenya definitely survives away from the places where tourists congregate. To visit the national parks accessed only by cars, there are several options:

☐ Cycle to the town nearest the park gate. Inquire about vehicles going into the park.

☐ Wait by the park gate. Ask to join with drivers whose vehicles have extra space and to share the car expenses.

☐ In Nairobi or Mombasa, select a tour that satisfies your time and budget needs from a variety of travel companies. Economic camping and luxury lodge tours are available (see the section *Travel Companies* in Chapter 11, *Getting Started in Nairobi*).

Outdoor enthusiasts generally agree that a few days of this sort of claustrophobic experience is quite enough.

CHAPTER 10

Security in Kenya

"Every head-man would be proud of a European visitor or resident in his territory, and there is perfect security for life and property all over the interior country."
   David Livingstone, 1857

Concerns for personal safety while exploring Kenya by bicycle and on foot focus on two questions:
- Is there a risk of being robbed or, even worse, attacked?
- Are the roads safe for cycling?

Relax. There is no need for excessive anxiety. A robbery or attack is highly unlikely if you exercise common sense. And yes, some roads are dangerous, but there are plenty of safe roads as well.

First-time visitors to Kenya may harbor misconceptions about the dangers of African travel. Such prejudices are nourished largely by an international press who fail to report positive news about the Third World. Westerners are told about violent eruptions on the continent and little else. It is not

Nairobi's Jamai Mosque. Kenya is greatly influenced by Muslim and conservative Christian values.

69

surprising that so many people are literally misinformed about the true nature of African peoples.

Some rather far-fetched though commonly held misconceptions about African travel are that bands of murderers may attack you, lions and tigers may chase you, and cannibals may boil you in their pots. All are exciting fantasies, but quite untrue. Areas of political turmoil and violence exist, but these are identifiable regions where aggression towards foreigners rarely surfaces. David Livingstone's impressions, recorded in his diaries while walking through much of the so-called Dark Continent in the 1850s, routinely refer to the honesty and generosity of the natives he encountered. My experiences 140 years later have been much the same. I am not a large or threatening person, yet I have never been robbed or attacked in Kenya. Why then do some tourists get robbed?

Security Precautions

"I began to perceive that a third world lay beyond, inside and intermingled with the two worlds I already knew of (…) a world that had its own laws and for the most part led its own life, but now and again, like a rock jutting up through earth and vegetation, protruded into ours … It was a world in which I was a foreigner…"

Elspeth Huxley, <u>The Flame Trees of Thika</u>, 1959

The major reason why foreigners are robbed when traveling in poor countries is that they unknowingly flaunt their valuables. Endemic poverty breeds economic crime. Purse snatchers and con men look for offguard tourists. Though most Kenyans are basically honest, hardworking people, you should take these precautions to insure that you are not victimized.

☐ Do not look rich or gullible. Avoid wearing expensive jewelry or watches. Keep only small amounts of money readily accessible. Place large amounts of money, passport, and plane tickets inside clothing. Do not tempt thieves by carrying loose handbags, cameras, or rucksacks which can be swiftly pulled or cut away from the shoulders. Avoid placing bags under tables or chairs without first securing these to your body in some way.

☐ Do not carelessly leave any goods unattended. In New York City or Amsterdam you would not dare to leave a bicycle or parcels unguarded. Practice similar caution in Nairobi and Mombasa.

☐ Robberies are more likely to occur in Kenya's larger cities. Such incidents in the rural villages are rare indeed. Observe these additional precautions, especially when staying in Nairobi or Mombasa.

☐ Never walk the streets after dark. Use taxis if you must travel. Do not rely on buses and *matatus* at night. Avoid crossing Uhuru Park in Nairobi during the day and especially at night. Carelessness can be costly or even embarrassing, as this example proves:
An Austrian man named Leo, who had lived in Nairobi for ten years, had too many beers one night at the Serena Hotel. Returning to his office via Nairobi's Uhuru Park, he was accosted by robbers. More than his money was taken, however. He left the park sans shoes, shirt, and trousers!

☐ If you are accosted by thieves, relinquish your goods. Don't resist; don't argue; don't threaten them.

☐ Your hotel room is your vacationer's home-away-from-home. However, more people have access to your hotel room than to your home. Carelessly leaving valuables unattended in hotel rooms is inviting trouble.

☐ Check the security of your hotel room before moving in. Do strong bars protect the windows? Do window latches function? Two locks should secure exterior doors, including one that can be activated only from within. When leaving items in a hotel safe, insist upon a receipt preferably signed by two supervisory persons.

To further allay unnecessary fears during foreign travel, review the safety precautions presented in *The Traveller's Handbook* (See Chapter 8, *Getting Along with the Locals*).

Advance Planning

A little advance planning can save a lot of headaches during holidays. Before departing, spend a short time completing these tasks.

☐ Make photocopies of all documents including passport, visa, and vaccination certificate. Place copies in each of

your bags. If a bag gets lost, these act as superb iden-
tifiers should an honest person want to return the bag.
Always keep copies separate from originals.

☐ Copy credit card numbers and emergency telephone
numbers for reporting stolen and lost cards. Do not bring
toll-free 800 numbers from the USA: these numbers do
not work from Kenya. Record the FAX numbers for
credit card companies. FAX services are available at the
Post Communications Centres in Mombasa and Nairobi.

☐ Register with your embassy upon your arrival in Nairobi. This is a particularly good idea if you are planning
a lengthy tour. Carry your embassy's Nairobi phone
number at all times (see *Embassies and Immigration
Authorities*, in Chapter 11, *Getting Started in Nairobi*).

Road Safety for Cyclists

To say that Kenya's drivers are not among the slowest or most
cautious in the world is a gigantic understatement. They seem
to thoroughly enjoy navigating vehicles, but their idea of a
good time makes the hair of visitors stand on end. Luckily, the
country has an abundance of scenic and uncongested byways.
Cycling on these roads is pure pleasure. For this reason, it is
important to follow the routes outlined in Chapters 14–19.

CHAPTER 11

Getting Started in Nairobi

"When in the future I retire
(So rung my fanciful reflection)
And find some land of heart's desire
Where everything will be perfection,
Motors shall vanish like a dream
And cycles be once more supreme."
    Guy Boas, "To a Bicycle Bell," 1933

Nairobi, 'The Green City in the Sun' is where most visitors start and end their safaris. Though Nairobi is more relaxed than most other large cities, it is nevertheless noisy and crowded. If you are an outdoor enthusiast you will not want to linger long.

Nairobi's Kenyatta International Conference Centre (KICC) also houses several different travel companies, making comparison shopping easy.

73

However, the capital offers services you may need before heading out to enjoy cycling and walking adventures. Suggestions for locating the essentials are detailed below.

Travel Companies

Some travel agencies act as brokers for many safari companies. Dealing with them helps to compare rates and services quickly. Beware, because agents are occasionally offered *chai* to push clients in the direction of certain tours.

° *Let's Go Travel*. Caxton House, Standard Street, Box 60342, Nairobi. Tel. 340331/213033. Popular, efficient broker for many companies. They are often busy and clients must wait in cramped quarters.

° *Kenyatta International Conference Center (KICC)* has several travel companies with offices close together facilitating comparison-shopping.

Airline Tickets

° *Fly Air*, on Koinange Lane, around the corner from Kenya Airways. Tel. 26176/338716. Helpful staff. National and international air reservations.

° *Just The Ticket*, at the Apic Centre, Westlands. Tel. 741755. Uncrowded, comfortable office. Pleasant staff headed by Mrs. Devani.

Extended Travel Tip

Air Canada has been offering a round-the-world air ticket in conjunction with Kenya Airways and Cathay Pacific. Reasonably priced. Purchase in Kenya. Valid six months.

National Park Camping Safaris

° *Gametrackers*. PO Box 62042, Finance House, Corner Banda/Loita Streets. Tel. 338927/22703.

° *Safari Seekers*. Jubilee Insurance Exchange House, Kaunda Street, Nairobi. Tel. 26206/334585. Ask for Zul. Friendly, helpful staff; good rates.

° *Special Camping Safaris Ltd.*, Gilfion House, Kenyatta Avenue, Box 51512, Nairobi. Tel. 338325/566142.

Post, Telephone, Fax

- *Kenya Post Communications Centre*. Haile Selassie Avenue, across the street from the Main Post Office. International phone calls, Fax, Telex. Open 24 hours.
- *Esther Wahome Bureau*. Jubilee Building, Wabera Street. Friendly, helpful staff. Fax, typing, photocopying. Open 8:00 am – 4:30 pm weekdays only.
- *The Copy Cat*. Sarit Centre. Fax, typing, photocopying. Open 8:30 am – 4:30 pm weekdays, 9:00 am – 12:00 noon Saturdays.

Post Offices

- Main Post Office. Haile Selassie Avenue. Poste restante, parcels, letters.
  Branches:
- Kenyatta International Conference Centre (KICC). Stamps only.
- Sarit Shopping Centre. Westlands. Stamps only.
- Lavington Shopping Centre. James Gichuru Rd. Stamps, parcels.
- Westlands Shopping Centre. Uhuru Highway. Stamps, parcels.

International Courier Services

- *DHL Worldwide Express*. International House, Mama Ngina Street, Nairobi. Tel. 335962; Kijabe Street branch, around the corner from the Norfolk Hotel. Tel. 337919. Credit cards accepted.
- *Chapex Ltd.*. Enterprise Rd., Industrial Area. Weekdays 8:00 am – 5:00 pm, Saturdays 9:00 am – 3:00 pm. Cheaper rates than DHL, but less conveniently located (take bus 11 from Haile Selassie Avenue).

Banks

Look for major banks along Kenyatta Avenue in the City Center. Suburban banks are found at Yaya, Hurlingham, Westlands, and Lavington Shopping Centres.

Banking Hours: 9:00 am – 12:00 noon or 1:00 pm weekdays. Barclays Banks also open Saturdays 9:00 am – 12:00 noon.

Embassies and Immigration Authorities

- *The Travel Index*, a free tourist publication available from travel companies in Kenya, lists all embassies, their telephone numbers, addresses, and hours
- *USA Embassy*. Corner Moi Avenue/Haile Selassie. Tel. 334141/50. Hours 8:30 am – 3:00 pm, weekdays.
- *British High Commission*. Bruce House, Standard Street. Tel. 335944/60. Hours 8:30 am – 11:30 am, 1:30 pm – 3:30 pm
- *Immigration Offices*. Nyayo House on Posta Rd. near Kenyatta Avenue is a yellow highrise building. All visa extensions are obtained here

Tourist Information Office

Located in Mama Ngina Street, opposite the front door of the Hilton International Hotel. Tel. 23285. Kenya Airways bookings, general tourist information.

American Express

American Express is called *Express Kenya Ltd.* and is located on Standard Street opposite Let's Go Travel. Open Monday – Saturday 9:00 am – 5:00 pm. Tel. 556688, Fax 557259, Telex 22274

Photo Developing, Camera Repairs

- *Africolour Labs*. Koinange Street; Tel. 23532. Sarit Centre; Tel. 743851. Box 30918, Nairobi. Hours 9:00 am–6:15 pm, Mon–Sat; 10:00 am–12:45 pm, Sundays at Sarit Centre only
- *Expo Camera Shop*. Mama Ngina Street. Tel. 336921. Hours 9:00 am – 6:00 pm, weekdays; 9:00 am – 1:00 pm, Saturday

Car Hire

- *Avenue Car Service Station & Car Hire*. Kenyatta Avenue. Tel. 332166. Hours 8:00 am–1:00 pm, 2:00 – 5:30 pm, Mon–Fri; 8:30 am – 12:30 pm Sat; closed Sunday
- *AVIS*. Kenyatta Avenue near African Heritage Shop. Tel. 336703/336794, Telex 22383. Hours 8:00 am–6:00 pm everyday. Jomo Kenyatta Airport, Tel. 822186. Open 24 hours

- *Glory Car Hire*. Diamond House, Tubman Road. Tel. 22910. Hours 8:00 am–6:00 pm Mon–Sat; 8:00 am – 1:00 pm, Sunday
- *Coast Car Hire*. New Stanley Building, Standard Street. Tel. 336570/25255, Telex 25345. Hours 8:00 am – 1:00 pm, 2:00 – 5:00 pm, Mon – Fri; 8:00 am – 1:00 pm, Saturday; closed Sunday
- *Hertz UTC*. Corner Muindi Mbingu Street/Kaunda Street. Box 42196, Nairobi. Tel. 331974. Hours 7:30 am – 6:30 pm every day. Jomo Kenyatta Airport, Tel. 822339. Desks in Hotels Intercontinental, Fairview, New Stanley

Nairobi Hotels

All prices quoted are in Kenya Shillings and were last confirmed in early 1991. Allow for approx. 10–15% increase per year.

Luxury:
- *Norfolk Hotel*. Harry Thuku Street, Box 40064, Nairobi. Tel. 335422, Telex 22559. Only luxury hotel with history and charm. During settler times this was the meeting place for adventurers and big White Hunters. Bed only prices: Single KS 2160, Double KS 2160

Moderate:
- *Fairview Hotel*. Bishop Road, Box 40842, Nairobi. Tel. 723211. A colonial style hotel with attractive gardens, 10 minute walk from the city center. Bed & breakfast: Single KS 600, Double KS 900
- *Jacaranda Hotel*. near Sarit Centre, Westlands, PO Box 47557, Nairobi. Tel. 742272-8. Bed and breakfast: Single KS 1150, Double KS 1150
- *Hotel Boulevard*. near the Norfolk Hotel, PO Box 42831, Nairobi. Tel. 27567/8/9. Good location near National Museum. Bed only: Single KS 900, Double KS 900, Triple KS 1150
- *Hurlingham Hotel*. Argwings Kodhek Rd., PO Box 43158, Nairobi. Tel. 721920/721001. 1–2 miles from city center. Quiet older establishment. 14 rooms. Bed and light breakfast: Single KS 900, Double KS 900
- *Oakwood Hotel*. Kimathi Street opposite New Stanley. Tel. 20592/3, 26234. Bed and breakfast: Single KS 900., Double KS 900, Triple KS 1150

Budget:
- *Methodist Guest House*. Oloitokitok Street (Take Bus 46 direction Gitanga Road). Tel. 567225. Pool, restaurant, some self-contained rooms. Full board: Single KS 900, Double KS 900
- *Flora Hostel*. 5 Ngong Avenue (take Bus 8,33 direction Ngong Rd.) PO Box 49865, Nairobi. Tel. 723013. Quiet surroundings. No small children allowed. Full board: KS 900 per person
- *Mennonite Guest House*. Church Road (Take bus 23 direction Church Road). PO Box 14894, Nairobi. Tel. 60264. Colonial charm, beautiful gardens in a quiet suburb. Full board: KS 250 per person

If these establishments are fully booked or you are traveling on a tight budget, resort to the following suggestions:
- *YMCA*. State House Road, Box 63063, Nairobi. Tel. 724117/724070. Restaurant, pool, dowdy rooms. Full board: Single KS 900., Double KS 900
- *Nairobi Youth Hostel*. Ralph Bunchie Road, Box 48661, Nairobi. Tel. 723012/721765. Friendly wardens. Bed only: KS70 per person. Membership Cards required, cost KS 900

Bus, Taxi, Train Terminals

Several bus and *matatu* terminals are located in the city center. The trick is discovering which terminal has transport to the desired destination! Do not look for printed bus schedules or a central transport kiosk. These do not exist. Simply ask a local — or two or three — and soon the proper terminal will be reached. Public transport vehicles have signs in their front windows giving a number and several place names along the route.

Buses:
- *Hilton Hotel Terminal*. Mama Ngina Street. Most local buses and *matatus* pass here. Kenyatta Avenue, near Nyayo House.
- *KBS Bus Station*. Temple Rd. Take care with your possessions when walking here.
- *Country Bus Terminal*. Between Pumwani Rd. and Landhies Rd. Recently, this has become the worst area of

Nairobi for walking. Avoid coming here on foot if possible, or walk with a local friend.

Taxis:

Taxis can be hailed anywhere. They are easily found by the major hotels. The Hilton, 6–80, and Intercontinental Hotels always have lines of available taxis. If you must go out at night in Nairobi, take a taxi and avoid public transport. Two reliable taxi companies are
- *Kenatco*, Tel. 338611/ 25123/21561
- *Jambo Taxis*, Tel. 27377

Book Stores

Reading books about Kenya while touring enriches your understanding of the culture immensely. Nairobi's bookstores have the best selection in the country. Visit them before starting the Grand Tours and Loops. Selecting paperbacks that can be traded or given away reduces the weight of your luggage.
- *Nation*. Kimathi Street, next to the New Stanley Hotel's front door. Crowded. Good book selection. Maps available. Other location is brand-new, around the corner from the New Stanley on Kenyatta Avenue. Same books, spacious shop. A third outlet is in Westlands Shopping Centre, next to Uchumi's Supermarket.
- *Select*. Opposite New Stanley Hotel on Kimathi. Roomy, good for browsing.
- *Book Corner Ltd.* and *Prestige Booksellers*. Opposite one another on Mama Ngina Street. Africana and paperback fiction.
- *Makueni Bookshop Ltd.*, Kaunda Street. Small bookstore near the New Stanley.
- *Textbook Centre*. Sarit Centre Outlet and Kijabe Street Outlet, around the corner from the Norfolk Hotel. Good for Africana literature, not good for popular fiction.

Shopping

Active travelers purchase souvenirs which are lightweight, unbreakable, and easily packed. Local wares meeting these standards are jewelry, precious and semi-precious stones, unframed batiks, fabrics, small baskets, and gourds.

Most of the crafts seen throughout Kenya can be purchased in Nairobi prior to departure. To complete a shopping list, plan to spend one day in the capital before leaving. Only shops selling quality merchandise are recommended. Visit City Market or the stalls near MacMillan Library for cheaper souvenirs.

- *Spinner's Web*. Kijabe Street, around the corner from the Norfolk Hotel. Hand-woven fabrics, rugs, wall-hangings, sweaters, jewelry, crafts
- *Kichaka*. Across the street from the Spinner's Web. Boutique with stylish dresses, leather handbags, jewelry.
- *Why Not?* Muindi Mbingu Street, lower level of Hotel 6–80. Handicraft boutique with fashionable T-shirts, handbags, jewelry.
- *Santa Fe*. Kaunda Street. Locally-designed women's clothes.
- *Sarang Art Gallery*. Standard Street. Paintings and carvings
- *Cottage Industries*. Standard Street. Clothes, batiks, paintings, jewelry.
- *The Craft Market*. Apic Centre, Westlands, Box 14249, Nairobi. Tel. 740421. Unique stoneware, rugs, leatherwork, ethnic jewelry, limited edition prints.

Mailing Parcels Home

The first choice for getting parcels delivered safely is to send the goods with someone who is flying to the destination. If this is infeasible and the post must be used, avoid Nairobi's Main Post Office. Personnel will almost certainly ask you to open all parcels for inspection. Instead, take parcels to a branch post office in Lavington Shopping Centre or Westlands Shopping Centre (see the section *Post Offices* in this chapter).

CHAPTER 12

Understanding Kenya

Millions of years ago the shape of what is now Kenya was changed in a spectacular fashion. A series of massive earthquakes and eruptions formed huge volcanoes and great depressions. Mt. Kenya and Lake Victoria, Africa's largest lake, resulted from these violent shifts. A major crack in the continent later joined with other fissures creating the Great Rift Valley.

Streams flowing into the valley floor from both sides of this gigantic fault formed a series of lakes. Forests disappeared in the lower, hotter areas and savanna grasslands took their place.

When the Rift was formed, a land bridge existed between East and West Africa. This allowed for the migration of wildlife and people when magnificent rain forests extended from west-

Less than an hour's journey from Nairobi's city center, Masai moran live in the Great Rift Valley. Massai are nomadic herdsmen who cling to their ancient traditions and dress. (photo Major Aussie Walker)

81

ern Africa to the Indian Ocean shores. Only 5–10,000 years ago, Kenya's original inhabitants, who were hunter-gatherers, wandered through this thickly wooded country.

Several thousand years later, the pan-African transmigration brought crop-growing Cushites to the region. The ancestors of the present 52 indigenous tribes were Cushite, Nilotic, and Bantu groups from all parts of the continent who arrived between 500 BC and AD 500. Next came the Arab and Persian traders who settled along the Coast and, finally, the Asians and Europeans.

By the mid-nineteenth century, both Britishers and Germans were interested in the East African Coast. The settlement of the interior, particularly the Rift Valley and Aberdare highlands, was forestalled until the 1880's by the Masai pastoralists. Early explorers who attempted to open the interior were Gustav Fischer (Fischer's Tower is in Hell's Gate National Park), Joseph Thomson (Thomson Falls is in Nyahururu), and Count Teleki.

Colonial Days

By the 1890's the Masai, weakened by years of civil strife, signed a treaty with the British. Soon after this agreement, the Mombasa to Uganda railway cut through the Masai grazing lands, its halfway point being where Nairobi stands today. With the completion of the railway, dubbed the 'Lunatic Express,' white settlers began to develop the fertile highlands north of Nairobi. Most of the land seized was taken from Kikuyu whose grievances later precipitated the Mau Mau revolt.

Lord Delamere from Cheshire, England, was the leader of the white settlement in the early twentieth century. Among the Europeans establishing coffee plantations were Karen and Bror von Blixen. In *Out of Africa*, Karen Blixen records her memories of this era. (See Loop 3 — *Nairobi Highlights*, in Chapter 14, *Nairobi and Environs* — a cycling tour to the Blixen home.) Rapid settlement of the so-called 'White Highlands' was interrupted by World War I. Under the Treaty of Versailles, however, the British were given a League of Nations' mandate to control Kenya. The white population of 9,000 in 1920 quickly grew to 80,000 by 1950, and the Kikuyu's discontent was on the rise.

A Kikuyu man born in 1892 as Johnstone Kamau, who later changed his name to Jomo Kenyatta, led the movement changing Kenya's political history. Under British rule, the Africans' plight had continued to worsen. By 1920, they had been banned from hotels and restaurants and could obtain only menial jobs within the colonial administration.

In 1953 African resentment exploded with the killing of a white farmer's cattle herd. In retaliation, the colonial government murdered 21 Kikuyu. The Mau Mau rebellion had begun, and its bloody events would continue until 1956 when the British declared victory. The final toll revealed that 13,500 Africans had been killed while only 100 whites had died. An additional 20,000 Kikuyu had been placed in detention camps, and Kenyatta himself was imprisoned for seven years.

Independence

Independence for Kenya did not come until 1963. Many whites had fled the country by this date, although Kenyatta himself

This Jomo Kenyatta statue, dedicated to the country's first president, stands in the courtyard near the Kenyatta International Conference Center.

asked them to remain. He appeared to hold no resentment towards them, saying that he wanted Kenya to represent the feasibility of different racial groups living harmoniously.

Kenyatta ruled as the country's first President until his death in 1978. His successor was Daniel arap Moi, a member of the Tugen tribe, who rules to this day. Since 1964, when Ronald Ngala and his KADU colleagues joined the KANU opposition party, has been the state's sole ruling party.

Harambee, meaning 'let's pull together,' became the slogan and spirit of mutual cooperation among the nation's peoples allowing progress to advance in several important areas. By 1970, a satellite ground station had opened in the Rift Valley, the International Airport had been extended to accommodate jumbo jets, and the thirty-three story Kenyatta International Conference Centre had been completed. Another major improvement increased health facilities from only 4,000 specialists in 1963 to 30,000 in 1989.

Kenya attracts hundreds of thousands of foreign visitors yearly. In 1987 Nairobi hosted the Fourth All Africa Games at the 80,000-seat Moi International Stadium. Kenya's Safari Rally, a grueling 2,500 mile event, lures participants from all corners of the globe. The tourist industry has become the country's most successful business and number one foreign-currency earner. For more than twenty-six years *harambee* and peaceful progress have made Kenya Africa's most stable country.

Part II
Recommended Routes

CHAPTER 13

Grand Tours and Loops

Cycling routes have been organized in this book as *Grand
Tours* and *Loops* to simplify
and personalize the planning
of your own safari. Grand
Tours are for those who have
at least two weeks in Kenya
and want to use a bicycle as
their main source of transportation. The most scenic and,
when possible, least conges-
ted roads have been selected.
Depending upon your fitness
and expertise in cycling, it is

possible to go virtually anywhere in Kenya by bicycle and/or
on foot. Long distance riders will want to review shorter Loops
and incorporate many of them into their itineraries.

Some travelers do not have the time or inclination to cycle
daily while on safari. Spending several days or even one
afternoon exploring Kenya by bicycle and on foot may be a
more realistic goal. Short tours, referred to as 'Loops,' vary in
length and difficulty, so that everyone can enjoy the experience
of cycling and walking 'on the wild side.' Remember that
Loops last from a few hours to a few days. They do not always
circle back to the starting point, though many Loops are circular routes. When they do not return to the starting point,
alternate transport is suggested for getting there.

Touring Regions

Grand Tours encompass five regions of Kenya, but Loops
explore six regions since one extra series of Loops provide
tours of Nairobi and its environs. Whether cycling the Grand

Tours or shorter Loops, your first task is to decide which of these regions to explore first:

∘ Nairobi and its Environs (Chapter 14)
∘ Central Highlands including Mt. Kenya (Chapter 15)
∘ Great Rift Valley Wonders (Chapter 16)
∘ Northwest Kenya and the Cherangani Hills (Chapter 17)
∘ Western Kenya and Lake Victoria's Islands (Chapter 18)
∘ Kenya's Coast, North and South (Chapter 19).

Each region has its distinctive landscape, peoples, and sights described in the Overviews preceding each Grand Tour.

Where to Start

How can you decide where to start? Dr. Clifford Graves, founder of the International Bicycle Touring Society, gives this advice:

"Decide what part of the country you want to see. Don't try to see it all. And don't hesitate to take the train if it suits your purpose. Lay out your route in general, but don't set up your overnight stops. That puts you under pressure. Play it by ear. Much more fun."

By carefully reviewing the descriptive highlights in the Overviews preceding each Grand Tour, you can decide which aspects of Kenya most intrigue you. Do you enjoy birdwatching and wild animals? Do you enjoy vistas of green hills, lakes, exploring backcountry roads, or camping? Is cruising along the coast your idea of a pleasant ride? Once a region has been selected, study the Grand Tour and Loop possibilities. Locating enough scenic routes to ride is not likely to be a problem. Choosing between the many exciting possibilities is what makes the task difficult.

Ride Ratings

Terrain and distance were considered when giving the Loops a Level of Difficulty Rating (referred to as Rating in the Loop descriptions).

☐ The **Easy** rating was assigned if the ride is less than 25 miles and covers mostly flat terrain with few or no challenging hills, Anyone who can ride a bicycle can enjoy these routes, even if you have not exercised recently. Families with children will find these Loops fun and not too difficult for any family member old enough to ride a standard size bicycle.

☐ The **Challenger** rating indicates that the route is longer than 25 miles and includes some hills, perhaps even steep inclines. These routes may cross rough roads with stony surfaces. Hence, riders must be adept in handling a bicycle in these conditions. If you are reasonably fit and bicycle occasionally, you will find that these Loops, as the name suggests, offer a challenge.

☐ The **Hardcore** tours, finally, were designed for those who ride regularly and far. You know who you are. Grinding up mountains and speeding down steep escarpments is your forte. You are in superb condition and probably think little of riding 75–100 miles a day. Even these cyclists may prefer to kick back and relax some days. Taking an Easy or Challenger Loop can provide that desired break.

Unless you cycle and walk frequently, beginning with Easy Loops and gradually sampling Challenger routes is a good plan. Starting off a vacation by 'overdoing it' can result in aching muscles and fatigue which can get an otherwise glorious adventure off to a bad start.

Deviations

Exploring is part and parcel of adventurous travel, and many excellent cycling routes could not be included in this book. Safety concerns are the chief consideration when trying uncharted routes. Attempting to check out road conditions and traffic congestion is often frustrating in Kenya. Keep asking until someone is found who genuinely knows what to expect on the road ahead.

Walking at Your Own Pace

Most of the suggested walks can be completed by everyone, though at different rates of speed. Whereas a fast, extremely fit walker may cover a particular trail in a few hours, others might stretch the same distance into a day's amble. It is important to walk at a pace that feels right. Competing with others for fastest times becomes distracting. By focusing on where you are — the birds flying overhead, the movement of animals in the bush, and the vibrant colors of the landscape — time considerations soon become meaningless.

High altitude sickness severely affects some individuals. When walking in altitudes above 3,000 m (10,000 feet), slow down and assess how you are feeling. If high altitudes have been a problem in the past, consult a doctor and your own common sense before tackling high-altitude walks.

Data Provided For Each Loop

In addition to the ride's **Rating** (Easy, Challenger, or Hardcore), these extras are provided to characterize the route more fully:

- **Description** of the people, area, and scenic highlights is briefly sketched.
- **Distance** the ride covered is given in miles and kilometers (kilometers are used more frequently on road signs in Kenya).
- **Terrain Characteristics** include flat, hilly, mountainous, or varied.
- **Road Conditions** define the road's surface (paved, dirt, gravel, sand, rocky, or mixed) and the prevailing traffic congestion (light, moderate, or heavy).
- **Accommodation and Meals** contains recommendations for lodges, campsites, guesthouses, and restaurants. In backroad communities, small lodges change often. Checking out the best available choice upon arrival is easily accomplished. Prices and exchange rates fluctuate rapidly; high and low season rates differ substantially. Rather than attempt to quote exact prices, hotels are ranked in price categories: Expensive, Moderate, and Budget. In general, the following applied at the time of writing (add 10–15% for each year after 1992): *Expensive* indicates US $50, UK £32 and above per person, *Moderate* indicates US $25–49, UK £16–30, and *Budget* indicates US $ 3–24, UK £2–15.
- **Walks** and optional **Sidetrips** are detailed. Take any or all of these options.
- **Route Directions** are outlined from a starting point to the finish.
- **Maps** for every Loop are furnished. These can be photocopied and put into the map pocket of a handlebar bag.

CHAPTER 14

Nairobi and Environs

Nairobi surprises many people who expect the entirety of Africa to be tropical jungle. It is a modern city by the continent's standards, with highrises, many restaurants and shops, and bustling sidewalks evidencing an international population. Today's Nairobi bears little resemblance to the town that Colonel Meinertzhagen, the famous wildlife authority, wrote about in his 1902 diary:

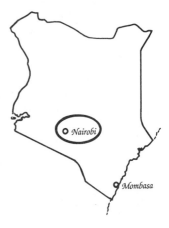

"The only shop is a small tin hut which sells everything (…) The only hotel here is a wood and tin shanty. It stands in the only 'street'."

This 'green city in the sun,' as Nairobi is often called, lies 87 miles (139 km) south of the Equator and 300 miles (480 km) west of the Indian Ocean. Nairobi's growth boom can be credited to the railway and pleasant climatic conditions. When George Whitehouse, general manager of the Uganda Railway, undertook the building of a 620-mile railway from Mombasa to Lake Victoria, he chose *Nyrobi* (in Masai, 'place of cool waters') as his main upcountry railhead. At 1650 m (5,500 feet), days are warm, with low humidity, and nights are cool. Temperatures rarely soar above 80°F (27°C).

When Independence was granted on December 12, 1963, Nairobi's population was only half a million people and its area 135 square miles (350 square km). By 1989 the area had swollen to 270 square miles (700 square km) and the population increased to over two million people. From the Embakasi plains in the east up the eastern wall of the Great Rift Valley in the west, from the Ngong Hills in the south to the foothills of the Aberdares in the north, the metropolis of Nairobi continues to expand.

Cycling Loops in the Nairobi region traverse the central portion of this vast area. Every Loop starts in or very near to the capital, making day trips or half-day outings possible. When touring by bicycle and on foot, one quickly senses the vast contrasts in housing and lifestyles of Nairobi's populace. Exclusive suburbs festooned with shaded gardens and security guards, where the affluent reside, do not bear the slightest resemblance to the crumbling shops and crowded sidewalks along River Road. Sleek Mercedes cars speed past men pulling heavy wagonloads of goods.

To the west towards the towns of Kikuyu, Banana Hill, and Limuru, farmlands owned by members of the Kikuyu tribe are densely planted with maize and bananas. Vast fields of white flowers are the cash-crop insecticide plant, pyrethrum. To the north is cool and vibrant green Kiambu, where coffee and tea estates abound.

Nairobi and its environs offer a rich variety of sights to cyclists and walkers: the suburb where Bror and Karen Blixen established a coffee farm in 1913 and which she was forced to abandon in 1930; the Animal Orphanage adjacent to Nairobi National Park where sick and orphaned animals are given care; Bomas of Kenya featuring traditional houses with hosts from Kenya's major tribes; the friendly giraffes at Langata Giraffe Centre; the highland forests of Kiambu; the interesting and informative Mitchell Farm called Kiambethu ; and even the infamous Muthaiga Country Club residential district. Finally, a tour of Nairobi's city center, either by walking any week-day or cycling on Saturday afternoons and Sundays when the streets are traffic-free should not be missed.

Nairobi Loop One
City Tour

Rating: Easy

Distance: 3–6 miles (5–10 km)

Terrain: Flat

Road Conditions: Paved. Heavy traffic (except Saturday afternoons and all day Sunday, when most shops are closed)

Points of Interest: Kenyatta International Cultural Centre (KICC), Parliament, City Hall, Jevanjee Gardens, French Cultural Centre, Goethe Institute, Mt. Kenya Safari Club, Norfolk Hotel, University of Nairobi, River Road, National Archives, Tourist Information Office, American Cultural Centre, Railway Museum. (Long Option): Uhuru Park, Arboretum, State House, All Saints Cathedral, New Stanley Hotel.

Sidetrip: National Museum (located at Museum Hill Roundabout opposite the International Casino, 10-minute walk from the Norfolk Hotel).

Starting Point: Harambee Avenue, in front of the Kenyatta International Cultural Centre.

Route Directions: Walk to Parliament Rd. and turn right. During weekdays the Parliament Buildings can be visited and the Memorial to Jomo Kenyatta is located on the grounds. At City Hall Way turn right passing City Hall, where the Inoculation Centre is located (a second Inoculation Centre is within the Jomo Kenyatta International Airport Complex). Turn left on Wabera Street and left again on busy Kenyatta Avenue.

After visiting the African Heritage Restaurant and Shop located further along Kenyatta Avenue, take Muindi Mbingu Street heading north. In two blocks the City Market is

A walking or cycling tour of Nairobi ends at the New Stanley's Hotel's Thorn Café, the city's most popular meeting place for tourists.

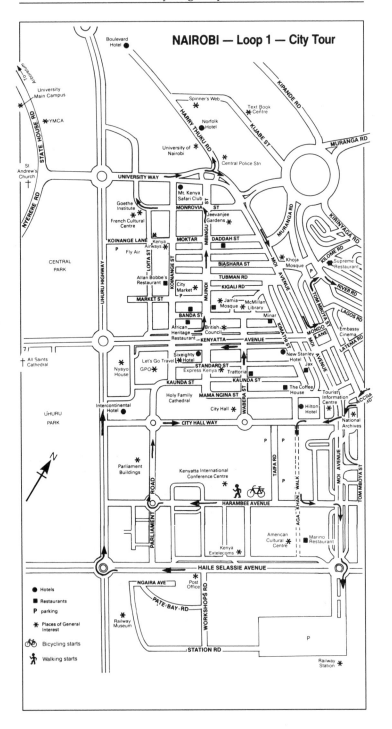

NAIROBI — Loop 1 — City Tour

reached (closed Sundays). Proceed north on Muindi Mbingu four blocks to Jeevanjee Gardens, bordered on the north side by Monrovia Street. Turn left onto Monrovia leading to the French Cultural Centre and Goethe Institute in two blocks.

Backtrack to Monrovia and turn left on Koinange Street. Continue one block to the Mt. Kenya Safari Club on the corner of Koinange and University Way.

Stay right on University Way and left at the next roundabout on Harry Thuku Rd. Large signs for the University of Nairobi and Norfolk Hotel mark this corner. Visit the Norfolk's courtyard for a nostalgic glance at the city's past. Exiting from the Norfolk Hotel, keep right and, at the first corner, turn right on Kijabe Street. The Spinner's Web and Kichaka Shop are nearby. A bit further on is the Textbook Centre which stocks a selection of Africaner books and paperback fiction.

Backtrack to the roundabout at University Way and Harry Thuku Rd. Turn left on University Way, which becomes Moi Avenue, a busy shopping district.

After a few blocks, turn left on Mondo Lane and left again on Tom Mboya Street. This long street ends at a major roundabout. The Supreme Restaurant, serving budget–priced Indian food, is on this roundabout. Turn right on River Rd. You are now among some of Nairobi's oldest buildings. This is a bustling area of working-class people. Be mindful of your possessions!

Continue along River Rd. to Accra Rd. and turn right. This road leads to Moi Avenue at the corner of the National Archives, Tourist Information Centre, and Hilton Hotel.

Travel east on City Hall Way passing the south side of the Hilton Hotel to Aga Khan Walkway. Turn left. The American Cultural Centre is one block opposite Marino and Tamarind Restaurants.

Aga Khan Walkway ends at Haile Selassie Avenue. Turn left on Haile Selassie and right on Moi Avenue which leads directly into the Railway Station. A right turn at the Station leads along the narrow Station Road to the Railway Museum where old locomotives, including the engine of the original 'Lunatic Express,' are stored.

At this point, take either the Long Option (detailed below) or backtrack to the Railway Station and along Moi Avenue passing the National Archives and turn left on Mama Ngina Street (Mama Ngina, one of Jomo Kenyatta's wives, is still living). In one block turn right on Kimathi Street. The New Stanley Hotel with its Thorn Tree Cafe is straight ahead.

☐ **Long Option:** Backtrack a short distance along Station Rd. to Workshop Rd. Turn left. Upon reaching Haile Selassie Avenue, turn left and continue to Uhuru Highway. Cross the highway, turn right, and proceed north on Kenyatta Avenue beside Uhuru Park.

At University Way, turn left and quickly right onto State House Rd. The main campus of the University of Nairobi, the Arboretum, and YMCA are found along this road. The State House itself is another 1.5 miles (2.5 km) ahead. When reaching State House, turn left and return to Kenyatta Avenue. A left turn at Kenyatta Avenue passes All Saints Cathedral and returns to Uhuru Highway. Cross Uhuru Highway and continue east on Kenyatta to Kimathi Street where the New Stanley is located.

Nairobi Loop 2
Where the Locals Live

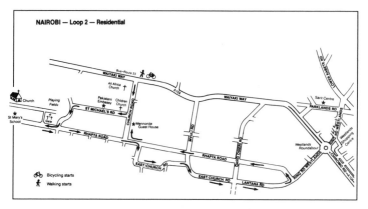

Description: Nairobi, like most large cities, has lovely residential suburbs generally missed by tourists. This short tour takes you to a beautiful school with an old stone church. Large estates reminiscent of colonial extravagance and modern townhouses line the streets. A unique Children's Church, where no adults are allowed unless accompanied by a child, and the peaceful gardens of the Mennonite Guest Home complete the tour. Cycle or walk this Loop; the distance is short.

Rating: Easy

Distance: 2.5 miles (4 km)

Terrain: Flat

Road Condition: Paved; light traffic

Points of Interest: St. Mary's School and Church; Pakistan Embassy, Residential estates, Children's Church, Mennonite Guest House

Walks: Convent and Girls' School grounds

Starting Point: Church Rd. at Waiyaki Way. [Take bus 23 from the City Centre to Church Rd., site of the All Africa Council of Churches unfinished structure. If cycling from the city centre along Uhuru Highway, use the roadside paths. Uhuru Highway becomes Chiromo Rd., then Waiyaki Way after the Westlands Roundabout].

95

Route Directions: Proceed south along Church Rd. to St. Michael's Rd. on the right. Follow St. Michael's Rd. past the Children's Church and Pakistan Embassy until its end at Rhapta Rd. Turn right on Rhapta and in one block the gate of St. Mary's School appears on the right.

Enter the spacious, peaceful school grounds passing the small cemetery. Take the left road which eventually crosses a stream where large Ibis and other waterbirds are often seen. On the hilltop the school and old stone church are situated.

☐ **Optional Walk:** Walk through the beautiful wooded grounds of the Convent and Girls' School adjacent to St. Mary's.

Backtrack to the school gate via the footpath across St. Mary's School. Turn left on Rhapta Rd. and continue past Church Rd. At East Church Rd. turn right. This beautiful lane eventually becomes Lantana Road and reconnects with Rhapta Rd.

Turn left on Rhapta Rd. Continue straight to Church Rd. Turn right. In one block is the Mennonite Guest House with its beautiful gardens and charming old buildings.

Giraffe Manor was built in 1932 by Sir David Duncan. The current owners founded the African Fund for Endangered Wildlife (AFEW) to save the Rothschild giraffe from extinction. (photo Richard Hartley)

Nairobi's Norfolk Hotel is the city's only luxury hotel with history and charm. During settler days, this was the meeting place for settlers and Big White hunters.

Backtrack along Church Rd. to Waiyaki Way. Take bus 23 to the City Centre or, if cycling, return via the following route.

☐ **Cycling Route to the City Centre:** From Church Rd. turn left on Waiyaki Way and, after several blocks, left again on James Gichuru Rd. Take Mzima Springs Rd. to the left. Again left on Mzima Lane, passing through a lovely residential area. Turn right at Riverside Drive. Follow Riverside all the way back to Uhuru Highway intersected at Museum Hill Roundabout.

Nairobi Loop 3
Nairobi Highlights

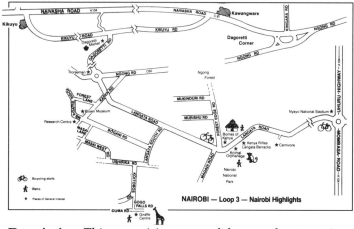

NAIROBI — Loop 3 — Nairobi Highlights

Description: This tour visits many of the popular attractions located close to Nairobi and allows cyclists a close look at several residential suburbs. The first stop is the Animal Orphanage adjacent to the Main Gate of Nairobi National Park. Because of heavy traffic on Langata Rd., Easy Option: cyclists may choose to arrive by bus. The Orphanage claims not to be a zoo, but rather an enclosure for young, sick, and stray animals who are nursed back to fitness before being allocated to the wilderness. Your donation helps the authorities to run this animal hospital.

Bomas of Kenya, a cultural center where people representing Kenya's major tribes have erected typical homes and sell their crafts, is a few kilometers further along Langata Rd. Beyond the Bomas, Ngong Forest encompasses many alluring acres of forest trails, though it probably should not be entered without the accompaniment of trusted locals. Inquire at the Forest Station for local 'guides' if you want to cycle or walk on forest trails. Bomas's quiet backroads lead to the Langatta Giraffe Centre.

Out of Africa familiarized the world with the suburb of Karen, where elegant estates occupy the Blixen's former coffee farm. The Easy-Does-It Loop ends at Karen Shopping Centre where lunch is available at the Horseman Restaurant and Pizza Garden. [Return to the City Centre by bus or taxi.] Challengers continue to Dagoretta, a working-class community, and a stark contrast to Karen's manicured estates.

Rating:	Easy	Challenger
Distance:	9 miles (15 km)	26 miles (43 km)
Terrain:	Flat	Hilly

Road Conditions: Paved; heavy traffic from Uhuru Highway to Bomas, along Langata Rd. Light traffic from Bomas onward.

Points of Interest: Animal Orphanage, Bomas, Ngong Forest, Giraffe Centre, Blixen Museum, Horseman Restaurant.

Walks: Animal Orphanage. AFEW Nature Sanctuary Forest Trail at Giraffe Centre; Blixen Museum.

Sidetrips: Ngong Forest Trails (with guides only).
Institute of Primate Research, Box 24481, Karen.
Nairobi National Park by taxi or hitching a ride near the Main Park Gate.

Accommodation and Meals: The Giraffe Manor offers very exclusive lunches, dinners, and rooms at steep prices. The mansion is spectacular, housing Karen Blixen's furnishings. Fees are a contribution (perhaps tax deductible) to the

Cycling with Rothschild giraffe. Once an endangered species, these can be visited at Giraffe Manor. (photo Richard Hartley)

AFEW Wildlife Foundation. Double US $400, Single US $300; Lunch US $35, Dinner US $50. Bookings: PO Box 15004, Nairobi; Tel. 891078.

Starting Point of Challenger Option: Langata Rd. at Uhuru Highway.

Route Directions: Ride along Langata Rd. (heavy traffic) on the dirt shoulder passing the Carnivore Restaurant sign and the Kenya Rifles (no photos). After three miles (7.6 km) is the Main Gate of Nairobi National Park.

☐ **Walk:** On the right is the Animal Orphanage which can be visited on foot.

Exit left onto Langata Rd. passing the Wildlife Club Hostel. After 1.3 miles (2.2 km), turn right on Forest Edge Rd. Enter Bomas of Kenya on the right.

Starting Point for Easy Option: Forest Edge Rd. off Langata Rd. at the entrance to Bomas of Kenya.

☐ **Walk:** Trails through Bomas lead to the housing compounds of various tribes. Meet the tribal representatives and purchase crafts if desired.

Exit Bomas, turning right on Forest Edge Rd. Cycle to the end of the paved road where the forest begins.

☐ **Sidetrip:** Ask at the forest station before cycling or walking into Ngong Forest.

Sightsee along Mukinduri Rd. and Murishu Rd. to view suburban residences. These roads do not connect, so backtracking is necessary. Backtrack passing Bomas. Turn right on Langata Rd. After two miles (3 km) turn left on Langata Rd. South at the small brown sign *Giraffe Centre*. Passing Tigaza College of Religion, Bogani Rd., and the VOK Transmitter, the road curves. Turn right on Ushirika Rd., then a quick left on Koitobos Rd. where another small sign points toward the Giraffe Centre.

Continue straight onto Gogo Falls Rd. At the road's end, turn left at the Giraffe Centre.

☐ **Walk:** A few Nature Sanctuary Forest Trails are near the Giraffe Centre entrance.

☐ **Sidetrip:** Continue on the road passing the Giraffe Centre. Stay left at the bottom of the hill. Superb views of the Ngong Hills appear on the horizon. Backtrack to the Giraffe Centre. Leaving the Giraffe Center, backtrack along Koitobos Rd. Turn left on Ushirika Rd., then right on Masai West Rd. and right again on Masai Lane (note sign marking Mwangaze House Jesuit Centre on the left). Left on Bogani Rd. which ends at Karen Rd.

When you reach Karen Rd., the Institute of Primate Research is left. Turn right towards the Karen Blixen Museum. Before reaching the museum, turn left on Mbagathi Ridge, a lovely wooded lane of large estates occupying the Blixen's former coffee farm. Turn right on Forest Lane where horse-riders are frequently seen. At Karen Rd. turn right to Karen Blixen Museum.

☐ **Walk:** Visit Karen Blixen Museum and walk through the adjoining grounds and former coffee farm. A small admission fee is charged. Leaving the museum, turn left on Karen Rd. After one mile (1.5 km) turn left on Langata Rd. to Karen Shopping Centre. Lunch or drinks are available at the Horseman Restaurant. This is where the Easy Option ends. Take bus 2 or 23 or taxi to Nairobi.

☐ **Challenger Option:** locate Dagoretti Rd. at the major intersection near Karen Shopping Centre. Cycle on Dagoretti Rd., passing Karen Bible School. After 3.2 miles (6.5 km) is Dagoretti Market, a slice of real Africa: small *dukas*, simple houses, and working- class people.

Remain on Dagoretti to Kikuyu Rd. Turn right on Kikuyu Rd. to reach Nairobi [or turn left to Kikuyu town. Buses 2, 24, 102 travel to Nairobi from here.]

Kikuyu Rd., direction Nairobi, ends after three miles (6 km). Turn right on Naivasha Rd. Heavy traffic. After 1.5 miles (2.7 km), turn left at Kingara Rd. At the large tree in the midst of an intersection, continue straight on James Gichuru Rd., a wide thoroughfare with a good cycling path. Lavington Shopping Centre ahead has a post office, bank, and bakery. A further 1.2 miles (2 km) is Mzima Springs Rd. See *Nairobi Loop 2*, this chapter, for the *Cycling Route to the City Centre*.

Nairobi Loop 4
Tea and Coffee Estates, Waterfalls, and a Settler's Farm

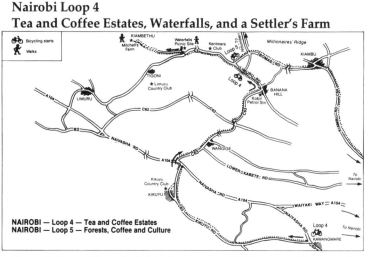

Description: Close to Nairobi are small Kikuyu villages evidencing no trace of the modern stylishness pervading Nairobi's city center. Surrounding these villages, large tea and coffee estates blanket the fertile hills en route to Limuru. A short distance from Limuru Rd. is the Waterfalls Picnic Site where horseriding, picnicking, and walking trails are available in a peaceful setting. During a visit to Kiambethu Tea Estate, Mrs. Mitchell, the daughter of a pioneer tea planter in Limuru, tells anecdotes of the family's lives. This is an opportunity to see a working farm and to enjoy lunch in the beautiful gardens. Advance reservations are necessary.

Rating:	Easy	Challenger
Distance:	13 miles (22 km)	30 miles (49 km)
Terrain:	Mostly flat with few hills	hilly
Road Conditions:	Paved, 1 mile of dirt road	Paved, dirt; moderate and low traffic

Sidetrips: Mitchell Farm, Tel. 0154-40756, or contact UTC (PO Box 42196, Nairobi. Tel. 331960) for reservations.

Accommodation and Meals:
- Kikuyu Country Club (budget rooms & restaurant) En route Limuru: Kentmere Club (luxury dining), Waterfalls Inn (budget snacks, Sunday buffet, picnic grounds).

Starting Point for Challenger Option: Kikuyu Rd. at
Naivasha Rd. [Follow Loop 3 directions in reverse to
Kikuyu Rd. or take Bus 102 to Kawangware trading center
on Naivasha Rd].

Route Directions: Cycle west on Kikuyu Rd. (C63) through
a picturesque area of large trees and small *dukas* (shops).
Notice the Kikuyu women shouldering heavy loads of firewood.

After 3 miles (4.8 km) is Dagoretti (Dagoretti Market is south
of Kikuyu Rd). Continue straight on Kikuyu Rd.

After another 5.5 miles (10.3 km), cross an overpass, and
quickly turn left into Kikuyu town.

Take the first right turn to Kikuyu Country Club. (This is a
locals' establishment, not a country club in the western
sense.)

Backtrack to Kikuyu Rd. and turn left. At Naivasha Rd. turn
left and quickly right on C63 at the sign, Waterfalls Picnic
Site. Cycle north on C63 through lush banana and
cornfields. Notice the blue haze over the distant hills. Light
traffic.

After 6.5 miles (11 km), C62 is met. Turn right and quickly
left on C63 once again. Excellent paved road through rural
countryside.

After 2.8 miles (4.5 km) where a Kobil Station is on the right,
turn left to Banana Hill trading center on Limuru Rd.

Starting Point for Easy Option: Banana Hill trading center
on Limuru Rd. [Buses and taxis from Nairobi travel to
Banana Hill.]

Follow Limuru Rd. west for 1.5 miles (2.6 km), noting the
sign, Kiambu 11.5 km, on Boma Rd. Do not turn.

Continue on Limuru Rd. 1 mile, passing the Kentmere Coffee Estate and Kentmere Club, where luxury dining is available to the public.

Brooke Bond's Mabrowkie Tea Estate is soon reached. This
estate was founded in 1903 when Thea Sinensis from India
was introduced. Pause to watch how teapickers, with large

baskets strapped on their backs, collect the leaves. Tigoni Study Centre is ahead on the left.

After 3.5 miles (5.5 km) turn right at the sign, Waterfalls Inn, 1 km. Follow the signs to the Waterfalls.

☐ **Walk:** Many hiking trails are found within the Waterfalls Inn compound. Explore the adjacent forest trails on foot. Backtrack to the road which intersects Limuru Rd.

☐ **Sidetrip and Walk:** Turn right 1.8 miles (3 km) passing the Limuru Girls' School to a sign, Mitchell, and a large white house on the left. This is Kiambethu Farm (the Kikuyu meaning is 'place of dancing'). A walking tour of the tea estate is possible with advance reservations.

Return to Nairobi by either (a) backtracking to Banana Hill and catching a bus or taxi to Nairobi; or (b) backtracking to Bomas Rd. and following Loop 5 to Kiambu and on to Nairobi; or (c) backtracking the Challenger Option route from Nairobi to Waterfalls Picnic Site.

Nairobi Loop 5
Forests, Coffee, and Culture

Description: This picturesque tour meanders through peaceful tea, coffee, and banana estates to Kiambu. Though only 10 miles (16 km) north of Nairobi, the cool forest setting of Kiambu is a refreshing contrast to the hurried pace of modern Nairobi. A walk through the forest and visit to Riuki Cultural Centre are relaxing and informative outings.

Rating:	Easy	Challenger
Distance:	6–12 miles (10–20 km)	16 miles (27 km)
Terrain:	Mostly flat	Flat, hilly
Road Conditions:	Paved, low traffic	Paved, low-moderate traffic

Accommodation and Meals:
° Nairobi: See *Nairobi Hotels* in Chapter 11, *Getting Started in Nairobi* for hotel and restaurant recommendations.
° Kiambu: Gold Star Hotel (budget rooms and restaurant)
° Kiambu Club (dining)
° Hotelis: picnic supplies

Starting Point for Challenger Option: Kikuyu Rd. at Naivasha Rd. [Follow Loop 4 directions to the intersection of Bomas Rd. and Limuru Rd. in Banana Hill.]

Starting Point for Easy Option: Bomas Rd. at Limuru Rd. near Banana Hill. [Refer to Loop 4, the sign on Bomas Rd, Kiambu 11.5 km. Buses from Nairobi travel to Banana Hill.]

Route Directions: Follow Bomas Rd. in the direction of Kiambu. One of the ridges soon passed is known as 'Millionaire's Ridge' because the rain and altitude blend perfectly to produce high quality coffee. This, presumably, has made some people very rich.

☐ **Sidetrip:** After 2.7 miles (4.5 km), turn left at the sign to Ndumberi and ride through dazzling green farmland bursting with multi-colored bougainvillea. Backtrack to Bomas Rd.

Continue straight 1.2 miles (2 km) to Turitu. Look for the charming stone church on the right after leaving the small trading center.

After 1.8 miles (3 km) a T-junction is marked with the sign *1 km, C63 to Kiambu; 16 km, C64 to Nairobi*. Turn right passing the Gold Star Hotel. Then turn left into Kiambu town, administrative capital of the district, surrounded by coffee plantations.

☐ **Walks:** Walk through Riuki Cultural Centre and Kiambu Market. Before proceeding into the Forest, ask to store bikes at the local police station. Ask police to provide a 'guide' (either a trusted local or an officer). Tip the guide after the walk. Easy Option: can either backtrack six miles (12 km) to Limuru Rd. or take a bus or taxi to Nairobi from the Kiambu station near the Market.

☐ **Challenger Option:** Cycle the 9.5 miles (16 km) from Kiambu to Nairobi on C64, Kiambu Rd. This ride is mostly downhill along a roadway bordered by forests. If time allows, *Loop 6 — Happy Valley Days*, as described below, can be completed before reaching Thika Rd. roundabout in Nairobi, where this tour ends.

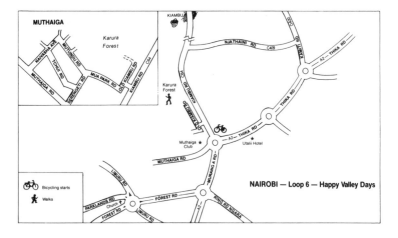

NAIROBI — Loop 6 — Happy Valley Days

Nairobi Loop 6
Happy Valley Days

Description: If you have read the book or seen the movie *White Mischief*, you will recall that Kenya's society-swingers during settler times were called the 'Happy Valley' set. These wealthy and often idle expatriates lingered at Muthaiga Country Club, presumably planning the evening's wild escapades.

Institutions change. Today this club, the ultimate symbol of Kenya's colonial past, is a conservative institution which prohibits business talk over lunch and women sitting at the men's bar. Visitors likely will not be allowed into the club without the sponsorship of a member. Touring the Muthaiga suburb is, however, open to all. If time allows, review *White Mischief*, cycle to Muthaiga and philosophize about the club's former habitues.

Getting a workout by walking or cycling in the Karura Forest is a good idea before going to the Utalii Hotel for lunch or drinks. Utalii is the training college for personnel involved in Kenya's tourist industry. The food and service is excellent and reasonably priced.

Rating: Easy (with Challenger Sidetrip)

Distance: 5 miles (8 km)

Terrain: Flat

Road Conditions: Paved; low traffic except 1 mile (2 km) from Muthaiga roundabout to Utalii Hotel

Accommodation and Meals:
- Nairobi: See Chapter 11, *Getting Started in Nairobi* for hotel and restaurant recommendations.
- Utalii Hotel (moderate rooms and restaurant)

Note: The Challenger Option may be combined with *Loop 5*.

Starting Point: Muranga-Kiambu-Muthaiga-Thika Rd. Roundabout.

Route Directions: Cycle north on Kiambu Rd. Turn left on Old Kiambu Rd. A quick right leads to the Forest Station road.

☐ **Walk:** At the Karura Forest Station, ask for a guide before walking or cycling on forest trails.

Backtrack to Old Kiambu Rd. and turn right on Mua Park Rd.

Continue straight to Mutundu Rd. until reaching Naivasha Avenue. Turn left. At Tchui Rd., turn left again, then right on Serengeti Rd.

A final left turn leads to Muthaiga Rd. Traffic increases here. Proceed with caution straight through the roundabout where the tour started.

Keep to the right side of Thika Rd., riding on the side road and avoiding the highway. After 1 mile (1.6 km), the Utalii Hotel is reached where the Easy tour ends.

☐ **Challenger Sidetrip:** Backtrack to the starting roundabout. Follow Kiambu Rd. north 7.5 miles (12 km). Turn right on C409, Njathaini Rd. After almost 3 miles (4.8 km), turn right on D400, Kamiti Rd. and soon turn right on Thika Rd. where moderate-heavy traffic conditions exist. Cycle on Thika Rd. using extreme caution 5 miles (8 km) west to the Utalii Hotel.

Cycling to the City Center: From the starting roundabout, cycle on Muranga Rd. for 0.6 miles (1 km) to the Forest Rd. roundabout. If traffic is heavy, walk your bike on the right side of Muranga Rd. Turn right on Forest Rd., cycling on the side road paralleling Forest Rd. At the next roundabout, the second left (before the Church) leads to Museum Hill and Uhuru Highway; the third left (after the church) leads along busy Parklands Rd. to the Westlands roundabout.

CHAPTER 15

Central Highlands and Mt. Kenya

The Central Highlands have always been of supreme political
and economic importance in
Kenya's history. A rather loose
definition of this region
embraces Thika and Muranga
in the south, the Aberdare
Mountains in the west, Nyeri in
the center, and Nyahururu and
Nanyuki in the north. Directly
west of Nanyuki is Mt. Kenya,
one of the world's largest free-
standing volcanoes, which
gave the nation its name.

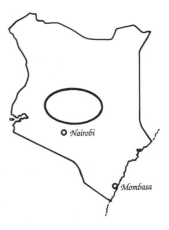

The richest farms in Kenya were created in the Central
Highlands by white settlers who cultivated this fertile region.
The countryside from Nairobi to Nyeri is all Kikuyuland and,
since it was their land the settlers largely took, it was the
Kikuyu who eventually organized the anti-colonial resistance
movement known as Mau Mau.

Ancestors of the Kikuyu had migrated into the region
between the sixteenth and eighteenth centuries from northeast
of Mt. Kenya. After clearing forests and planting crops, they
established peaceful trade with the hunter-gatherer people
already living in the highlands. However, Kikuyu and Masai
both valued cattle highly and were continually raiding one
another's herds.

Despite these clashes, the two cultures had much in common including the tradition of advancing in status while growing older through age-sets. Both tribes practiced circumcision
of young men and women (many clans still do), marking their
transition into adulthood. After circumcision boys could grow
long hair and dye it with ocher (a Masai fashion to date) and
stretch their ear lobes with heavy weights and cylindrical ear
plugs.

Mt. Kenya, according to Kikuyu beliefs, is Ngai's (God's) home. Hence, their houses were always built with doors opening towards the sacred mountain. Jomo Kenyatta, a Kikuyu and Kenya's first president, elaborated on these beliefs in his treatise entitled *Facing Mt. Kenya*. This book, available at many Nairobi bookstores, makes for interesting background reading of Kenya's history.

In Kikuyu villages a family may occupy three or more traditional round thatched huts. Kikuyu women carry large loads of firewood held upon their backs by a leather or sisal thong passed around the forehead. Women do most of the work in the *shambas* (family garden plots) and men, if they own much land, may have several wives to cultivate their holdings.

Early settlers' experiences in the Central Highlands were memorialized by Elspeth Huxley in *The Flame Trees of Thika* and *Out in the Midday Sun: My Kenya*. During her childhood years, the Blue Posts Hotel beside Chania Falls in Thika was a meeting place for settler-farmers including her father. Del Monte's pineapple plantations now cover much of the farmland near Thika. Rising 7,041 feet (2,166 m), Ol Doinyo Sapuk (Masai for 'the mountain of the buffalo') is always visible from Thika and from the Komo Rock Rd. leading to Tala. This mountain is a national park where many bad-tempered buffalo reside, and travel to the summit along the poorly maintained road is discouraged without accompanying rangers.

Beneath Ol Doinyo Sapuk roar Fourteen Falls. These 90 ft. (27 m) deep cataracts are a spectacular feature of the Athi-Sabank-Galana River.

Muranga, further north, was established by the British in 1900 as Ft. Hall, an administrative outpost. This bustling town, situated on a cliff above the Tana River, contains the Memorial Cathedral Church built in memory of Kikuyu who fought and died for Independence. Between Muranga and Nyeri, at Mugeka, is a grove of wild fig trees which Kikuyu claim as their Garden of Eden. They believe that their god, Ngai, ordered the mother and father of all Kikuyu to settle here. Mumbi, the mother, brought forth nine daughters who later founded the nine Kikuyu clans.

In Nyeri, situated at 5,750 feet (1,770 m), is the Outspan Hotel with its beautiful gardens and considerable facilities including tennis, fishing, and horseriding. Lord Baden Powell, founder of the Boy Scout movement, spent his last years at the Outspan where his cottage can be visited today. From the

Outspan, safaris leave for the famous Treetops game-viewing lodge in Aberdares National Park. A watering pond with salt licks attracts buffalo, elephant, giant forest hog, and antelope to the doorstep of Treetops. Since all transport to Treetops Lodge is by hotel cars, cyclists are at no disadvantage. All guests — cyclists and car travelers — are transported to the secluded Treetops Lodge via hotel vehicles. Advance reservations through Nairobi and Mombasa travel agencies are recommended.

Mt. Kenya, Africa's second largest mountain, was first seen by a European in 1849. When the missionary, Krapf related his stories of a snow-covered mountain straddling the equator to other foreigners, he was not taken seriously. In 1883 the Scot, Joseph Thomson, confirmed the mountain's existence, and Sir Halford Mackinder reached the highest peak, Batian, in 1899. Thirty years later Nelion, the second highest peak, was finally conquered.

Many Kenyan tribes have retained their ancient traditions and lifestyles. An Akamba woman in Tala Market.

Thomson's gazelles, affectionately known as Tommies, photographed in the Central Highlands.

Climbing Mt. Kenya

Four main routes lead to Mt. Kenya's summits: the Naro Moru, Chogoria, Burguret, and Sirimon. The Naro Moru route, shortest and most popular, offers lodging and camping at the Meteorological Station and Mackinder's Camp, a lovely stone building with windows opening to glorious vistas of Nelion and Bation. Arrangements for the required guide and optional porters can be made at Naro Moru River Lodge or upon arrival at the park entrance gates.

Grand Tour
Central Highlands and Mt. Kenya

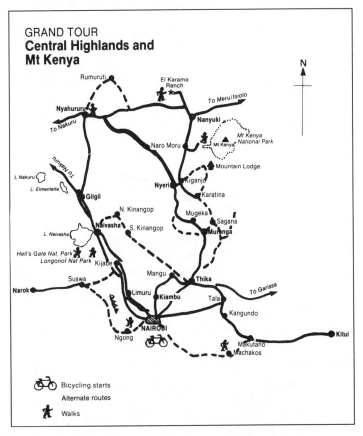

Starting Point: in Nairobi at the Kiambu-Thika Rd. Muthaiga Roundabout.

Route Directions: Cycle north 10 miles (16 km) to Kiambu on C64, Kiambu Rd.

From Kiambu, continue 18 miles (30 km) on C64 to Mangu. At Mangu, turn right towards Thika reached after 9.5 miles (16 km). From Thika, follow *Central Highlands Loop 3* from the starting point of the Hardcore Option to Nyeri. Distance 27 miles (45 km).

Upon reaching Nyeri, cycle north 27 miles (45 km) to Naro Moru. Follow Loop 4 to the start of the Naro Moru Route for climbing Mt. Kenya. Distance 9.5 miles (16 km).

From Naro Moru, cycle north 15 miles (25 km) to Nanyuki. Either follow Loop 5 route to El Karama Ranch and Nyahururu (93 miles, 157 km) or extend this route: When leaving the Ranch and returning to Naibor Rd., turn left and cycle northwest 30 miles (50 km). When reaching C77, turn south. In 25 miles (40 km) Rumuruti is reached. Continue south another 36 miles (60 km) to Nyahururu.

From Nyahururu, take the *Central Highlands Loop 6* route to Gilgil. Distance 40 miles (67 km).

Leave Gilgil heading south via the old Nakuru–Naivasha Highway running through the town to an overpass where the railroad track crosses the new A104 highway. Cycle or walk your bike a short distance along the railroad track to connect with the Old Naivasha Rd. Eventually this road runs parallel to A104 leading to Naivasha town. Distance 20 miles (38 km).

☐ **Sidetrip:** See the *Grand Tour — Rift Valley Wonders*. Reverse the route from Lake Elmenteita south to Suswa and Ngong.

From Naivasha town, select one of the first two options to reach Nairobi or the last one to reach Thika:

° Continue on the Old Naivasha Rd. passing the turn for Longonot Volcano and National Park to the sign, Kijabe, on the left. Follow the dirt track, eventually becoming steep, to Kijabe town perched on the hilltop. Follow Kijabe Rd. until it connects with A104. Ride south on A104 until the exit for Limuru, a left turn after a shallow lake. From Limuru, return to Nairobi on the old Limuru Rd. Distance 60 miles (100 km).

° Continue on the Old Naivasha Rd. 15 miles (25 km) until reaching the sign *Narok*. Turn right on Narok Rd. and continue 18 miles (30 km) until Suswa. Cycle south 48 miles (80 km) on the dirt road to Ngong. Follow Ngong Rd. 12 miles (20 km) to reach Nairobi.

° From Naivasha town take the North Kinangop Rd. Upon reaching North Kinangop in 18 miles (30 km), turn south

Three species of giraffe live in Kenya, and cyclists see them all. This Masai giraffe wanders near the roadside amongst acacia trees.

to connect with the White Sisters Rd., reaching Thika after 54 miles (90 km).

☐ **Sidetrip:** From Thika, take the Garissa Rd. to the Fourteen Falls exit which leads south to Tala (see *Central Highlands Loop 2*). Either follow the route of *Central Highlands Loop 1* beyond Tala (continuing to Kangundo, Kivani, Makutano, Kakutano, and Kitui) or follow the Komo Rock Rd. west to Nairobi from Tala.

Central Highlands Loop 1
Savannas and Sacred Hills

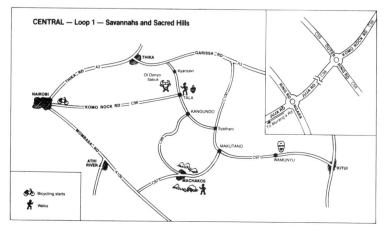

Description: Open spaces with long vistas characterize the Komo Rock Rd. route to Tala in the heart of Kambaland. If the trip were made for no reason other than visiting the picturesque Tala Market, it would still be worthwhile. Seated women gently rock large gourds of milk until ready to serve in mini-gourd cups, *mzees* carve bows and arrows, crowded tables are stacked artfully with colorful fruits and vegetables, and goats wander everywhere. The market is delightfully authentic.

On the horizon looms Ol Doinyo Sapuk, the Buffalo Mountain, shaped like a sleeping whale. To the south is Machakos surrounded by the Ukambani Hills. Masaku, a famous Kamba chief who foretold the coming of the railroad, lived atop Kiima-Kilwe Mountain, now a sacred place for the Kamba tribe.

Rating: Challenger [Easy Option: catch the bus towards Tala. Get off halfway and continue by bicycle.]

Distance: 67 miles (111 km) total. Nairobi to Tala-48 miles (7 km) Tala to Kagundo 4.5 miles (8 km) and Kagundo to Machakos 22 miles (37 km)

Terrain: Flat to Kagundo, then steep hills

Road Conditions: Paved, dirt track from Tala to Machakos (dry season only); low traffic

Sidetrips:
- Climb Kiima-Kilwe and other sacred mountains surrounding Machakos.
- Cycle to Wamunyu to visit the origin of Kenya's wood carvings (18 miles, 30 km east of Machakos).
- Cycle to Kitui where the Nzambani Stone is found. A legend holds that one who walks around it seven times, turns into the opposite sex. (80 miles, 130 km east of Machakos)

Accommodation and Meals:
- Tala: Kwa Joe Tourist Lodge (budget rooms and restaurant)
- Machakos: Five Hills View Lodge (budget rooms with inspiring views of sacred hills and restaurant)
- Kitui: Kithomboani Hotel, Gold Spot Motel (budget rooms)
- Ramrook's Place (locals' eatery)

Starting Point: 9 miles (15 km) east of Nairobi on C98, Komo Rock Rd. Take any bus towards Tala and ask to alight when traffic dwindles. [Cycling out of Nairobi is possible, but the traffic is fierce. If you insist, take Ring Rd. Ngara east at the Forest-Muranga Rd. roundabout. Ring Rd. Ngara and Juja Rd. meet at a second roundabout. Turn left on Juja and continue east through Eastleigh, a poor Nairobi suburb, and along a rough, dusty road to the Starting Point.]

Route Directions: Cycle east on smooth and lonely C98, Komo Rock Rd., to Tala. Upon entering Tala, turn left to Kwa Joe Tourist Lodge. A right turn leads to the picturesque Market.

☐ **Walk:** Walking around Tala, through the market and beyond the city center, provides a fascinating look at an area that has only slightly succumbed to modernization.

Continue on the road passing Tala Market to the sign Kagundo Market. Turn left to visit this peaceful little village built in a forest, completely removed from the tourist trail.

☐ **Easy Option:** Continue to Machakos by bus from Kagundo.

Backtrack to the highway and turn left. After two miles (3 km) the paved road ends and a dirt track begins. Use this road during dry seasons only.

Continue to Machakos passing small villages giving the impression that the clock has been turned back at least one hundred years. Kathaana, at first glance, appears to be a ghost-town; its residents move ever so slowly.

Before you, too, get lulled into somnolence, continue 10 miles (16 km) until the paved road begins.

Steep climbs and breathtaking views now prevail. Test the bicycle's brakes before the nine-mile (15 km) descent into Machakos.

[From Machakos, buses to Nairobi, Kitui, or Mombasa leave regularly.]

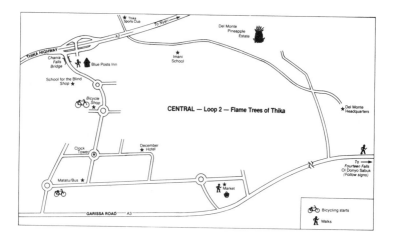

CENTRAL — Loop 2 — Flame Trees of Thika

Central Highlands Loop 2
The Flame Trees of Thika

Description: Thika, a rather unprepossessing community, is well known historically for several reasons. Churchill camped near the town's Chania Falls in 1907, Queen Elizabeth II had lunch at Thika Sports Club in 1983, and Elspeth Huxley recounted her glowing childhood on a Thika farm in *The Flame Trees of Thika*, published in 1959:

"We were going to Thika, a name on a map where two rivers joined. Thika in those days — the year was 1913 — was a favorite camp for big-game hunters and beyond it there was only bush and plain. If you went on long enough you would come to mountains and forests no one had mapped and tribes whose languages no one could understand."

The old Blue Posts Hotel where Huxley's family borrowed cups and met other white settlers is still in business calling itself the New Blue Posts Hotel. The roar of Chania and Thika Falls are heard from the hotel grounds. Huxley recalled her arrival to this place:

"We came at last to a stone bridge over the Chania river, newly built, and considered to be a great achievement of the PWDS. Just below it, the river plunged over a waterfall into a pool (...) and further on it joined the Thika. This meeting- place of rivers was a famous hunting-ground; not long before, Winston Churchill had slain a lion there (...) A hotel had been started just below the falls. It consisted of a low-roofed, thatched grass hut whose veranda posts were painted blue and gave the place its name."

A tour of Thika is primarily a nostalgic journey into the Kenya of 80–90 years past. Pineapple estates now cover much of the surrounding land, though many old coffee farms remain. In 1988 when I lived in Thika, I could still follow hippo tracks along the river bank near my home. The area is no longer thick with game but, in October and November, the flame trees faithfully burst forth with brilliant reddish-orange blossoms.

Rating: Easy

Distance: 8–10 miles (13–17 km)

Terrain: Flat (one hill beyond the Blue Posts)

Road Conditions: Paved, dirt; low traffic

Sidetrips and Walks:
◦ Ol Donyo Sabuk National Park
◦ Fourteen Falls
◦ Thika Market
◦ Chania Falls

Accommodation and Meals:
◦ Thika: New Blue Posts Hotel (moderate rooms and restaurant); December Hotel (budget rooms and restaurant)

Starting Point: The *matatu* stall near Barclays Bank in Thika. [Buses and *matatus* leave Nairobi from Racehorse Rd. arriving in Thika in 45 minutes]

Route Directions: From the street before Barclays Bank, cycle towards the Market, reached after 0.5 mile (0.8 km).

☐ **Walk:** Thika's Market is large, bustling with traders, and delightfully authentic — a good place to browse and people-watch. Locate the pottery section near the rear where Kikuyu women sell their wares.

Backtrack from the Market to the town center's clocktower. Here is a good place to pause and, while looking down the wooden- pillared streets, reflect upon the Thika of 80 years past.

Near the clocktower is December Hotel where local business persons have morning and afternoon tea.

Straight ahead of the clocktower is one of the best bicycle shops this side of Nairobi.

Further on the same road is the School for the Blind. Its craft shop is well worth a visit. The selection may be large or small; one never knows. Meeting the students is always rewarding.

Directly ahead of the School for the Blind is the Chania Falls Bridge which Huxley described. After crossing the narrow bridge, turn right. Up the hill is the New Blue Posts Hotel.

☐ **Walk:** From the New Blue Posts Hotel, walk along the river and to the base of the falls.

Leaving the New Blue Posts Hotel, cycle north on A2 — Thika Highway. At the hilltop on the left a sign points to Thika Sports Club where Queen Elizabeth II stopped for lunch. Golf, tennis, swimming, and dining are available, though you might need a temporary membership. Ask upon arrival for the current policy.

The road passing Thika Sports Club continues to a coffee estate with superb views across the valley. Backtrack to A2. Cross A2 to the dirt road leading into pineapple plantations. Signs on the corner indicate Imani School. Backroads crisscrossing the plantations offer quiet traffic-free rides with good birdwatching and views of Mt. Kenya on clear days. Do not pick the pineapple! Askaris (guards) are watching. Follow the signs towards Del Monte Headquarters but keep right to Garissa Rd., when this road's traffic is in view.

Upon reaching A3, Garissa Rd., turn left for a Sidetrip to Fourteen Falls or turn right returning to Thika town center and the *matatu* stall.

☐ **Sidetrip and Walk:** Follow Garissa Rd. 10 miles (17 km) to a sign indicating the turn to Fourteen Falls. In 1 mile (2 km) the Falls are reached where the Athi River cascades down towards the Indian Ocean. Askaris (guards) are posted in this area the last few years due to some nasty muggings. To be on the safe side, cycle to Fourteen Falls in a group and ask an *askari* to accompany the group through the forest to the foot of the falls. Limited picnicking supplies are available from *dukas* and *hotelis* at the turning near Garissa Rd. or in Ol Doinyo Sapuk trading center. If interested, hitch a ride with any vehicle traveling into Ol Doinyo Sapuk National Park, 'where the buffaloes roam.' Backtrack to Thika town.

Central Highlands Loop 3
Kikuyu Garden of Eden and Treetops Excursion

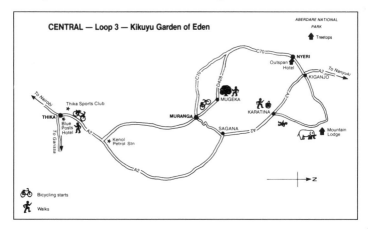

Description: North of Thika is the heart of Kikuyuland. At Mugeka lies Mukuruene wa Nya-Gathanga, meaning 'tree of the building site.' According to Kikuyu legend, this grove of wild fig trees is the Garden of Eden. Further North the market at Karatina is unusually colorful with baskets of fruit skillfully displayed on bright kangas spread on the ground.

From Nyeri, a short ride to the Outspan Hotel carries you fifty years into Kenya's colonial past. The gardens and splendid stone structure hint of the luxuries early settlers could enjoy. A sidetrip to Treetops Lodge in Aberdere National Park leaves from the Outspan; transportation is provided. Advance reservations for Treetops are recommended.

Rating:	Easy	Challenger
Distance:	17 miles (28 km)	57 miles (95 km)
Terrain:	flat, hilly	hilly
Road Conditions:	Paved moderate traffic	paved; low–moderate traffic

Rating: Hardcore

Distance: 99 miles (165 km)

Terrain: Hilly

Road Conditions: Paved; low-moderate traffic

Sidetrips: Treetops Lodge in Aberdere National Park

Accommodation and Meals:
- Nyeri: Outspan Hotel (expensive rooms and restaurant);
  Green Hills Hotel (moderate rooms and restaurant)
  White Rhino Hotel (budget rooms and restaurant)
- Karatina: Tourist Lodge (budget rooms and restaurant)

Starting Point for Hardcore Loop: Thika at the historic New Blue Posts Hotel. Cycle north 7 miles (12 km) on the moderately busy Thika highway to the Kenol Petrol Station. Turn left towards Muranga. Continue 18 miles (30 km) to Muranga. Follow the Challenger's route from here.

Starting Point for Challenger Loop: Muranga near the Post Office. D428 runs directly in front of the Post Office. Cycle 11 miles (18 km) to Mugeka. The sacred fig grove is beyond the community on the slopes of the Aberderes.

☐ **Walk:** Meander into any of the enchanting valleys below this mountain massif. Walking trails abound. Continue on D428 west to connect with C70 north to Nyeri. When entering Nyeri, continue straight passing Al-Falah Mosque. The road divides; staying right leads to the city center, left to the Green Hills Hotel, and straight to the Outspan Hotel.

Starting Point for Easy Option: The Outspan Hotel in Nyeri. (Take a bus from Nairobi to Nyeri or come with a travel company van for the Treetops safari.)

☐ **Sidetrip:** From the Outspan, turn right on the highway cycling towards the Aberdere National Park Entrance Gate. Backtrack to the Outspan.

Leave Nyeri via A2 south, arriving in 17 miles (28 km) to Karatina.

☐ **Walks:** 1.5 miles (2.5 km) before reaching Karatina (1.2 miles, 2 km, after the Mountain Lodge sign), turn left on the dirt road leading through farmland to a coffee estate. A walking tour of Karatina town and the colorful market is well worthwhile.

☐ **Options when Leaving Karatina:**
a. cycle or bus to Thika or Nairobi
b. cycle to the Mountain Lodge, 12 miles (20 km) from

Karatina. The forest reserve near the Lodge is home to buffalo. Check with locals about the safety of this road for cycling or walking before starting towards Mountain Lodge. Consider hitch-hiking the last few miles.

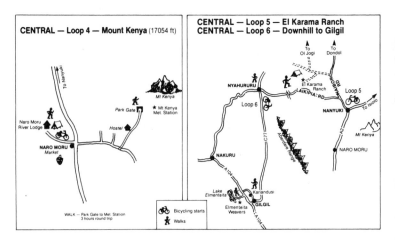

Central Highlands Loop 4
Mt. Kenya, Africa's Second Highest Volcano

Description: Mt. Kenya, the second highest mountain on the African continent after Kilimanjaro, dominates the Naro Moru vicinity. Though the bulk of the mountain straddles the Equator with twin peaks, Bation and Nelion, soaring to 17,054 feet (5199 m) and 17,036 feet (5192 m) respectively, Pt. Lenana at 16,300 feet (5199 m) is the summit most visitors reach. Climbing the others requires technical equipment and expertise. When cycling from the Naro Moru River Lodge to the Park Gate, this impressive mountain is constantly in view. Whether you climb to the top, walk to the Met Station, or ride only to the Park Entrance Gate, being near the shimmering beauty of these snow-white peaks is a highlight of any Kenya safari.

The walk to the Met Station passes through bush and bamboo forests where elephant and buffalo roam. Meeting one of these animals is a real possibility in this area, and is a confrontation you should try to avoid.

Rating: Easy

Distance: 19 miles (32 km) roundtrip

Terrain: Flat

Road Conditions: Dirt and gravel (best during the dry season); low traffic

Sidetrips and Walks:
° Birdwatching walks near the Naro Moru River Lodge, especially rewarding in early daylight hours
° Walk from the Park Gate to the Met Station

Accommodation and Meals:
° Naro Moru River Lodge (expensive rooms, cottages, or budget camping and restaurant)
° Met Station (*bandas*, which are simple shelters, or camping. Bring all food.)

Starting Point: Naro Moru River Lodge

Route Directions: Return to the A2 highway from the Lodge. On the opposite side of the highway is a sign *Mt. Kenya National Park Naro Moru Route*. Follow this dirt road.

After 2.2 miles (3.7 km) a T-junction is reached with a sign *Mt. Kenya Porters & Guides*. Turn right.

After only 0.6 miles (1 km) a sign marks the left turn to the Catholic Mission and the office of guides and porters. Sodas and basic food supplies are available in this small trading center.

Continue on the main road 0.7 mile (1.2 km) further until the sign, Mt. Kenya Park Entrance, signals the left turn.

Cycle 6 miles (10 km) from the sign to the Park Gate.

☐ **Walk:** At the Park Gate, discuss with the Rangers the possibility of cycling onto the Met Station and storing bikes there (if you plan to climb Mt. Kenya), or leaving the bikes at the Park Gate to take the three-hour roundtrip walk to the Met Station.

Backtrack to the Naro Moru River Lodge via the same route.

☐ **Sidetrip:** Instead of turning left at the sign, Mt. Kenya Park Entrance, continue straight. Ahead are miles of dirt road with farms, small villages, few people, peaceful quietude, and the presence of Mt. Kenya.

Central Highlands Loop 5
El Karama Ranch and Wildlife Tracking

Description: Nanyuki at 6,400 feet (1950 m) is situated on the banks of Ngare Nanyuki, meaning 'Red River' in the Masai language. The place has the feel of a small frontier town with the original (1938) old Settlers' Store on Main Street. Private El Karama Ranch, situated 25 miles (42 km) to the northwest, offers superb views of Mt. Kenya, especially in the early morning. Wildlife on the ranch abounds: bushbuck, giraffe, waterbuck, impala, gazelle, kongoni, zebra, and even lion, leopard, elephant, hyena, and buffalo.

Cycling all the way to the campground and cottages is possible. Guides lead you on tracking expeditions to discover more wild animals. Arrive before noon to avoid the afternoon rains.

Rating: Challenger [Easy Option: Cycle 25 miles [42 km] to El Karama Ranch. Backtrack to Nanyuki the following day]

Distance: 93 miles (157 km) in two days

Terrain: Flat, hilly

Road Conditions: Paved, dirt; low traffic

Tala's market is delightfully authentic. These Kamba women weave sisal baskets.

Sidetrips and Walks:
∘ Horseriding (English saddle) is available to experienced riders at El Karama Ranch.
∘ Birdwalks and game tracking at the Ranch.

Accommodation and Meals:
∘ Nanyuki: Sportsman's Arms (budget rooms, camping, and restaurant)
∘ Josakt Hotel (budget rooms and restaurant)
∘ El Karama Ranch (*bandas*, camping; bring all food; bedding, cooking utensils are available)

Starting Point: Nanyuki

Route Directions: Leave Nanyuki via the Laikipia Rd. (direction Nyahururu)

After 5.5 miles (9 km), turn right on Naibor Rd.

Continue 14 miles (23 km) until three signboards saying *Ol Joagi — No Shooting* appear. Turn left. In six miles (10 km) the campsite and bandas are reached.

When leaving El Karama, backtrack to the Laikipia Rd. Turn right on Laikipia Rd. and continue 52 miles (84 km) to Nyahururu

Central Highland Loop 6
Downhill to Gilgil: Thomson Falls, River Walks, and History

Description: Nyahururu town was formerly called Thomson's Falls after the same explorer who gave the Tommy gazelle its name. Waters of the Ewaso Narok River thundering over the narrow cliff passage create Thomson's Falls. To reach the base of the falls requires hiking down into a dramatic gorge over wet and slippery rocks.

The ride from Nyahururu to Gilgil skirts the western side of the Aberdare Mountains. If you have not completed the Rift Valley Loops, the Kariandusi Prehistoric Site and Lake Elmenteita are easily accessible from Gilgil. For the exciting history of Galbraith Cole's home, Kekopey, on Lake Elmenteita's shores, refer to the Rift Valley overview in Chapter 16.

Rating: Easy

Distance: 40 miles (67 km)

Terrain: Downhill

Road Conditions: Paved; low traffic

Sidetrips and Walks:
° Walk through Marmanet Forest and along the banks of Ewaso Narok River near Thomson's Falls
° Walk through Kariandusi Prehistoric Site
° Cycle to Lake Elmenteita and Galbraith Cole's home (now Elmenteita Weavers)

Accommodation and Meals:
° Nyahururu: Thomson's Falls Lodge (moderate rooms, camping, and restaurant)
° Lake Elmenteita: Elmenteita Weavers (drinks and light snacks)
° Naivasha: La Belle Inn (moderate rooms and popular restaurant)
° Nakuru: Hotel Waterbuck (moderate rooms and restaurant)
° Gilgil: Salama Lodge (budget rooms)

Starting Point: Nyahururu at the Thomson's Falls Lodge

Walks:
° Hike into the gorge to the base of Thomson's Falls. Proceed with caution along this trail, especially if the rocks are wet.

○ A second walk starts from Thomson's Falls Lodge gate. Exit left over a bridge. Turn left again down into the forested valley on the opposite side. Follow the Ewaso Narok River more than a mile (several kilometers) downstream. Colobus monkeys and chameleons are often spotted in this area. Cross the river on fallen trees and return to the lodge.

Route Directions: Cycle south on C77 to Gilgil. This is not a strenuous ride; the road is paved and mostly downhill. Even inexperienced riders should have no problems covering the 40 miles (67 km).

☐ **Easy Option:** Return from Gilgil, where buses south to Naivasha or Nairobi and north to Nakuru and beyond leave frequently.

☐ **Sidetrips and Walks:** From Gilgil, cycle to the Kariandusi Prehistoric Site only a few miles away. Again, the ride is almost completely downhill. Short and long walking trails pass through the archaeological digs.

Leaving Kariandusi, continue to A104. Turn left and cycle one mile (1.5 km) to the small sign *Elmenteita Weavers*. Turn right at the sign towards the lake and follow the dirt track to the Weavers. The shoreline of Lake Elmenteita, abundant with birdlife and unusual conical hills, offers superb walking country, uncluttered by tourists.

CHAPTER 16

Great Rift Valley Wonders

As described in Chapter 12, a series of massive earth movements and eruptions created mighty volcanoes and formed huge depressions in the earth. millions of years ago. The 17,054-foot (5199 m) peaks of Mt. Kenya and the largest inland body of water in Africa, Lake Victoria, resulted from these explosive shifts. When a major crack joined with other fissures extending almost 4,000 miles (6,400 km) from Lake Baikal in Russia down through Lebanon and the Red Sea to Mozambique, the Great Rift Valley was born.

Within Kenya, the valley floor rises from 650 feet (200 m) above sea level at Lake Turkana to 6,200 feet (1,908 m) near Lake Naivasha, descending abruptly before entering Tanzania to the south. Great cliffs rise more than 5,000 feet (1,520 m) above the floor.

Kenyan park ranger Simon Kilongo Tully borrowed a bicycle to ride with American cyclists to Lake Bogoria's hot springs. In the background is the Laikipia Escarpment.

The first glimpse of the Great Rift Valley is unforgettable. After cycling out of a thin forest belt, suddenly, 2,000 feet (615 m) beneath a sheer escarpment, is the greatest valley in the world. Another 30–60 miles (50–100 km) away, the opposite dark purple wall rises against the blue sky. The floor itself is tawny red during the dry season and silvery-green after the rains.

Dozens of volcanoes have erupted in the Rift, but the greatest was Kilimanjaro. Though many of these volcanoes are extinct, thirty are active or semi-active while countless boiling springs still exist. Mt. Longonot, a dormant volcano, is visible upon reaching the first Rift Valley overlook north of Nairobi. From the crater of this 9,111 foot (2,804 m) mountain wisps of steam eddy up among the trees. Nearby is Mt. Suswa, a 7,733-foot (2,357 m) dormant volcano, whose crater has a deep moat in its center and large lava tubes to explore. Overlooking the town of Nakuru to the north, Menengai Volcano possesses the second-largest caldera in the world. Intrepid cyclists can tackle the steep road from Nakuru to the crater rim for a hearty workout.

Crossing the Rift Valley by bicycle offers views of many wild and distinctive natural features: soda lakes, arid plains, steep escarpments leading to cool highlands, sand rivers, and glimmering granite cliffs. A series of lakes, strung like pearls across the valley floor were formed when streams flowed into the basin from both sides of the gigantic fault. The southern-most of these lakes within Kenya's boundaries is Lake Magadi. To the north is Lake Naivasha, then Elmenteita, Nakuru, Bogoria, Baringo, and, finally, Lake Turkana in the undeveloped Northern Frontier Province bordering Ethiopia.

The German naturalist Gustav Fischer was the first European to locate Lake Naivasha in 1883. Hostile Masai warriors caused him and other early explorers to flee the area quickly. Later, Joy Adamson lived on Naivasha's shores at Elsamere where she nurtured the lioness Elsa and wrote the wildlife classic *Born Free*. Excellent wine is made from grapes grown on farms opposite Lake Naivasha's Crescent Island. This island's crescent shape is actually the exposed tip of a crater rim. Boat trips to the island are available from either Lake Naivasha or Safariland Lodge. While walking on Crescent Island, gazelle, waterbuck, giraffe, hippo, and hundreds of birds, including the five-foot-tall Goliath Heron, are easily spotted.

The Masai tribe moved down into the Rift Valley in the seventeenth century, establishing their rule over the region. In times of drought, the Purrko and Damat clans came to Lake Naivasha's shores with great cattle herds and Kakonyuki people also came from the slopes of Mt. Kenya. Civil wars broke out among these groups which eventually weakened the Masai's control.

The arrival of white settlers further diminished Masai influence in the Lake Naivasha vicinity. A second treaty with the British in 1906 forced Masai to move south of the railway line to the top of the Mau range and beyond. Europeans quickly flocked to the fertile lands near the lakeshore to set up extensive farms and ranches. Agricultural development, advancing at an accelerated pace, has created a sizable horticultural and floricultural center near the lake. Large flower farms creating a sea of brilliant red, orange, and white blossoms between Lake Naivasha and Hell's Gate National Park are especially beautiful.

Hell's Gate National Park is one of two national parks in Kenya allowing cyclists and walkers to enter. Njorowa Gorge within Hell's Gate was the ancient outlet for Lake Naivasha. A walk through this gorge lined with sheer red cliffs leads to inviting hot springs, a perfect miniature spa for tired cyclists. Fischer's Tower is one of several volcanic plugs within the park which technical climbers enjoy scaling. The movies *Sheena — Queen of the Jungle* and, more recently, *Mountains of the Moon* were filmed here which provides an explanation for the occasional fiberglas boulder. For birdwatchers, the star attraction of Hell's Gate is the lammergeyer, a rare bearded vulture. Large herds of gazelle, eland, zebra, giraffe, and buffalo graze within the park and, yes, the occasional lion as well.

Lake Elmenteita, one of the Rift's soda lakes, often assumes the appearance of a silvery blue birthday cake fringed with shimmering pink icing when thousands of Greater and Lesser Flamingos nest along its shores. Galbraith Cole's home, Kekopey, is a short distance away. Cole, an early white settler and Lord Delamere's brother-in-law, shot a Kikuyu (presumably intentionally), and for this was deported from Kenya. Soon he returned surreptitiously, disguised as a Somali. Crippled with arthritis and blind in one eye, he committed suicide at Kekopey in 1928.

Nakuru, at an altitude of 6,000 feet (1,847 m), lies to the north and is the focal point for visits to Nakuru National Park. Bordered on the west by one wall of the Rift, the 73-square mile park is a sanctuary for Rothschild's giraffe and the endangered black rhino. Python, leopard, hippo, and more than 450 recorded species of birds also live within the park's boundaries. Visits to the park can be arranged in Nakuru town via taxi or tour company.

Leaving Nakuru, the Rift Valley drops 3,000 feet (925 m) to the semi-desert lands surrounding Lake Bogoria. Only 31 miles (51 km) from Nakuru at the foot of the Laikipia Escarpment, Bogoria is the most beautiful and least visited of the Rift Valley lakes. At an altitude of between 3,280 and 5,250 feet (1,000–1,600 m), the lake's western shores steam with thermal jets and geysers. Cyclists can circle the lake while viewing graceful gazelle, tiny dikdik, leaping duikers, elusive greater kudu, and several million flamingo.

Lake Baringo is dramatically set in a branch of the Rift with the Kamasia Block in between. Submerged hippos, snapping crocodiles, and more than 500 species of birds, some permanent residents and others migrating from the European winter, populate Baringo's shores. The Njemps people who speak a Masai dialect inhabit this area. They survive by fishing and livestock herding and, unlike most pastoral people, they break the taboo on fish eating. Their dinghies, made from saplings of the fibrous ambatch tree which grows at the lake's southern end, appear half-submerged in the water.

Beyond Lake Baringo, after the paved road ends, a rough trail leads straight down into the heart of the northern Rift. The Suguta Valley is one of the hottest places on earth, and the once-occupied town of Kapedo was finally abandoned in the 1970's. Carry plenty of water if cycling in this direction. Because of sweltering temperatures and the scarcity of water, riding long distances on bicycle into the extreme Northern Frontier is impractical.

Returning south towards Nairobi, the Aberdare Mountains border the eastern side of the road. Within the 10,000-foot (3,080 m) Aberdare National Park are exotic trees and plants like gums, alpine bamboo, groundsel, and lobelia. Wildlife includes elephant, buffalo, waterbuck, eland, serval cats, rhino, and colobus monkeys. From the Kinangop Plateau, a steep road leads to one of the park gates. Accompanied by armed rangers, walking within the park is an exciting safari adventure.

Grand Tour
Rift Valley Wonders

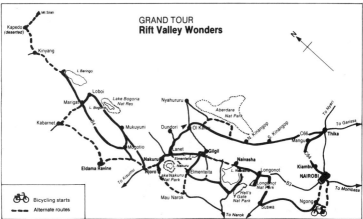

Starting point: Ngong town [reached by bus from the Hilton Hotel Bus Terminal in Nairobi or by cycling Langata Rd. until reaching Ngong Road in the suburb of Karen, and following Ngong Rd. to Ngong trading center], is a distance of 12 miles (20 km). See *Nairobi Loop 3 — Nairobi Highlights*, (Chapter 14), which starts on Langata Rd. A recommended option is to follow *Rift Valley Loop 1*, below, before continuing north.

Route Directions: From Ngong trading center, locate the dirt road leading north to Suswa. After 48 miles (80 km) B3, Narok Highway is joined.

☐ **Sidetrip and Walk:** Nearby Suswa Volcano has a rough dirt track leading all the way to the top. Cycling and walking along this road are permitted. Turn right onto B3 and continue 18 miles (30 km) to Old Naivasha Rd. Turn left, soon passing the entrance to Longonot National Park in six miles (10 km).

☐ **Sidetrip and Walk:** Turn into the dirt track at the sign *Longonot National Park*. After 3.5 miles (6 km) the Ranger Station is reached. To hike to the rim of Longonot Crater takes about one and a half hours from the trailhead; walking around the crater rim adds another two hours. Camping in the park is permitted. Bring food (the only food sold by the Rangers is live chickens); drinks are available. Park entrance fees are collected. Continue nine miles (15

135

km) on the Old Naivasha Rd. to Naivasha town, where several hotels and restaurants are available, La Belle Inn being the most popular.

From Naivasha town, follow signboards to Moi Lake Rd. South. Approximate distance to accommodation below is 12 miles (20 km).

Accommodation near Lake Naivasha:
- Lake Naivasha Lodge (expensive rooms and dining)
- Safariland Lodge (expensive rooms, camping and dining)
- YMCA Camp (*bandas*, camping; no dining)
- Hell's Gate National Park (camping with no facilities)
- Fisherman's Camp (*bandas*, camping; no dining)
- Elsamere (moderate rooms and dining)

☐ **Sidetrips and Walks:** Follow Loop 2 to visit Hell's Gate National Park, Elsamere, Crescent Island and Green Crater Lake.

Stay on Moi Lake Rd. South which eventually becomes Moi Lake Road North. Take the dirt road following the old railway line on the east side of Lake Naivasha to reach Elmenteita trading center. Distance 36 miles (60 km).

☐ **Alternate Route:** If roads are wet or paved roads preferred, backtrack to Naivasha town and continue north to Nakuru along the Old Naivasha Rd. which parallels the new highway for some distance. After nine miles (15 km) you must leave the roadway; cycle or walk your bike beside the railway track on the overpass of the new highway. Continue on the Old Naivasha-Nakuru Rd. (paved) to Gilgil. From Gilgil, cycle north to Nakuru]

From Elmenteita trading center, consider two options to reach Nakuru:
- Cycle west to Mau Narok and north through Njoro to Nakuru. Distance 42 miles (70km); or
- Follow the track leading to the east side of Lake Elmenteita; continue north on the highway (moderate traffic) leading to Nakuru. Distance 36 miles (60 km).

Leaving Nakuru, cycle north on B4 (light traffic) passing Mogotio and Marigat to reach Lake Baringo. Distance 84 miles (140 km).

☐ **Sidetrip and Walks:** See *Rift Valley Loop 4 — Lake Baringo: Birds, Hippos, and Crocodiles* in this chapter.

Backtrack 12 miles (20 km) from Lake Baringo to Marigat. Continue south a short distance to the sign, Lake Borgoria National Reserve. Turn left at the sign and follow *Rift Valley Loop 3 — Millions of Flamingos*.

☐ **Sidetrip (Hardcore):** This is the most difficult cycling tour in Kenya. From Marigat, turn west 18 miles (30 km) to Kabarnet. From Kabernet, cycle south 42 miles (70 km) towards Eldama Ravine. This road joins C55 south to Kampi ya Moto. Distance 22 miles (37 km). Take B4 south 12 miles (20 km) to Nakuru.

From Lake Bogoria, cycle to the south end of the lake to Mukuyuni Gate. Follow the dirt track leading south to Nakuru. [Alternate Route: rejoin B4 and backtrack to Nakuru.] Distance 55 miles (90 km).

☐ **Sidetrip:** In Nakuru, tour Lake Nakuru National Park by renting a private car, taxi or joining a travel company safari.

From Nakuru, take A104 south to Lanet. Turn west at Lanet on the road to Dundori and Ol Kalou. Distance 20 miles (33

A sense of man's origins lingers in Kenya. A touring cyclist watches the sunrise on the shores of Lake Baringo in Kenya's Great Rift Valley.

km). From Ol Kalou, cycle east on the road leading towards the Aberdare Mountains. Distance 8.2 miles (17 km).

☐ **Sidetrip:** Continue east to the Aberdare National Park Gate, reached via a well-paved and very steep road. Ask the Rangers for an armed escort to walk inside the Park. Following elephant and buffalo trails through the park is intensely exciting if at times equally frightening.

When the road forks (C77 north leads to Nyahururu), take C69 south to South Kinangop. Distance 66 miles (110 km).

From South Kinangop C66, the White Sisters Rd. is lined with white mountain lilies and leads to Thika. Distance 30 miles (55 km).

Leave Thika via the road to Mangu. Distance 10 miles (16 km). After reaching Mangu, take C64 south 19 miles (30 km) to Kiambu.

From Kiambu, a ride 10 miles (16 km) south on C64 ends in Nairobi.

Rift Valley Loop 1
Legendary Ngong Hills

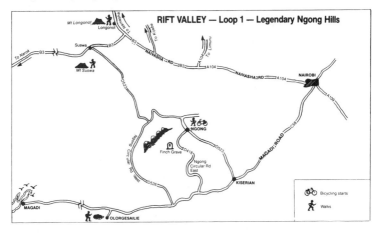

Description: West of Nairobi is Masailand and the Ngong Hills, memorialized by Karen Blixen in her book, *Out of Africa*. One chapter, entitled *The Grave in the Hills*, recalls romantic afternoons she spent picnicking there with Denys Finch-Hatton.

"I remembered how Denys had told me that he wished to be buried in the Ngong Hills (...) There was a place in the Hills, on the first ridge in the Game Reserve (...) I myself (...) had pointed out to Denys as my future burial-place (...) he remarked that then he would like to be buried there himself as well."

The site of Finch-Hatton's grave is now on Kikuyu farmland, and visits are allowed. Blixen's recollections suffice to explain why a visit to this place is unforgettable:

"Once when we were camped in the hills to look for Buffalo, we had in the afternoon walked over to the slope to have a closer look at it. There was an infinitely great view from there; in the light of the sunset we saw both Mount Kenya and Kilimanjaro."

The four knuckle-shaped peaks of the Ngongs can be easily crossed on foot, though obtaining an escort from the Ngong Police Station is advisable.

Olorgesailie Prehistoric Site is 25 miles (42 km) west of Ngong trading center along the Magadi Rd. *Bandas* (basic shelters) are available, but water and food must be brought to the site. From Olorgesailie, another 28 miles (48 km) further west after descending through the Ol Keju Nyiro Valley, is Lake Magadi, one of the Rift Valley's soda lakes. Camping is the only option for accommodation at Magadi, unless staying in a local's home. Several daily buses travel between Magadi, Ngong, and Nairobi.

Rating: Easy [Challenger and Hardcore extensions]

Distance: 22 miles (38 km)

Terrain: Hilly

Road Conditions: Graded dirt, paved; low traffic

Sidetrips and Walks:
- Walk across the four Ngong Hills.
- Bus to Olorgesailie Prehistoric Site. Walk the site's trails (option: stay in one of the *bandas*; lions are heard roaring during the night). Climb nearby Esakut Mountain.
- Bus to Lake Magadi where the lakeshore has abundant birdlife; cycle beyond the lake.

Accommodation and Meals:
- Ngong Hills: Bring a picnic lunch. Drinks are available at Denys Finch-Hatton's grave, Ngong and Kiserian trading centers.
- Camping in the Ngong Hills: arrange with private families to camp on their farms
- Nairobi hotels and restaurants are 45 minutes away by bus

Starting Point: Ngong trading center.

☐ **Walk:** Before starting to walk across the four Ngong peaks, stop at the Ngong Police Station to inquire about an escort and bicycle storage.

Route Directions: Cycle south on Ngong Circular Rd. East (the road passing the Police Station joins this road) towards the grave of Denys Finch Hatton. A small sign marks the entrance to a stony lane leading to the Kikuyu farm. Admission is charged.

Continue south on Ngong Circular Rd. East to Magadi Rd. Turn left to Kiserian.

☐ **Walk:** Visit the Kiserian Market and meet Masai people of the area.

From Kiserian, take the Magadi Rd. west. [Challenger and Hardcore Extensions start here.]

☐ **Easy Option:** Locate a sign on the right pointing to a dirt road, the continuation of Ngong Circular Rd. This sign faces the opposite direction; it can be read only if approaching from the west. Turn right on the Ngong Circular Rd. West which returns to Ngong trading center where the Easy Loop ends. [Bus to Nairobi, Olorgesaille, or Magadi.]

☐ **Challenger Extension:** Follow the Easy route, but do not turn right on Ngong Circular Rd. West from Magadi Rd. Instead, continue straight on Magadi Rd., 25 miles (42 km) across the Rift Valley floor until reaching the sign for Olorgesaille. Turn left on the dirt road to the prehistoric site and *bandas*.

☐ **Hardcore Extension:** Follow the Challenger Extension. After leaving Olorgesaille, continue southwest on Magadi Rd., 25 miles (42 km) across the Rift Valley floor to Lake Magadi. This is a hot ride, so carry sufficient water to last from Kiserian to Lake Magadi. Beyond the lake, dirt roads lead through sparsely populated country having abundant wild animals and birds, excellent camping sites, and hiking trails into the hills.

Rift Valley Loop 2
Hell's Gate and Lake Naivasha

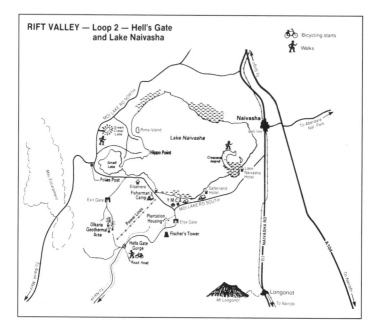

Description: Cycling among herds of plains animals and walking into deep granite gorges are some of Hell's Gate National Park's many attractions. A few miles away is Elsamere, Joy Adamson's former home where she lived with the lioness Elsa. The best afternoon tea in Kenya (complete with an entire table of pastries) is served at Elsamere. Crescent Island, a private reserve for wildlife and birds, can be explored on foot. Finally, Green Crater Lake shimmers amidst an acacia forest encircled by cliffs. Masai farms extend beyond the lake, a quiet, isolated retreat to cycle, walk, think, or write.

Rating:	Easy	Challenger
Distance:	16–20 miles (27–34 km)	40–45 miles (66–75 km)

Terrain: Mostly flat (one hill in the park)

Road Conditions: Dirt, paved; low traffic

Sidetrips and Walk: Boat trip to Crescent Island for a walk 'on the wild side.' Make arrangements for a boat at Safariland or Lake Naivasha Lodge.

Accommodation and Meals:
- Safariland Lodge (expensive rooms, camping and restaurant)
- Fisherman's Camp (budget *bandas*, camping; no food)
- YMCA Camp (budget *bandas*, camping; no food — the nearest trading center is 1.5 km away)
- Lake Naivasha Lodge (expensive rooms and restaurant)
- Elsamere (moderate rooms and restaurant)

Starting Point: Elsa Gate of Hell's Gate National Park [*Matatus* and buses pass this way from Naivasha town.]

Route Directions: Upon entering the park gate, follow the main road through the park. At Fischer's Tower, a road to the left is a pleasant diversion for large herds of zebra, eland, and kongoni are sometimes found in this direction.

☐ **Walk:** After five miles (8.5 km), look for a sign marking the Ranger Post on the left. The Post's exhibit explains the geology of the region. The largest volcanic cone within Hell's Gate is reached via a path from the Post. Rangers can point out the trail leading down into the gorge where a pleasant walk along its floor leads to hot springs.

The main park road passes through the geothermal area where roaring steam jets burst forth. The exit gate is straight ahead.

After exiting the park, watch for speedbumps before reaching Moi Lake Road South. Turn right on Lake Rd. and continue 2.5 miles (4 km) to Elsamere for afternoon tea, or to watch the video on Joy Adamson's life, visit the museum and shop, or relax with colobus monkeys in the lovely gardens overlooking Lake Naivasha.

Continue on Moi Lake Rd. South to Fisherman's Camp or Safariland.

☐ **Sidetrip and Walk:**
- Boat trips to Crescent Island leave from Safariland and Lake Naivasha Lodge. Advance reservations are recommended. Ask to spend several hours on the island.
- At Fisherman's Camp, self-paddle boats are for hire. Exploring the reeds along the shoreline by boat is never dull since many birds and hippo live there.

☐ **Challenger Extension:** Follow the basic route until exiting Hell's Gate National Park.

Turn left on Moi Lake Rd. South and continue six miles (10 km). After passing the Police Station on the left, continue 1.2 miles (2 km) to a dirt road on the right. Opposite this turn is a sign for a retreat center. There is no sign for Crater Lake. Turn right into the dirt track and, after only 75 yards (69 m), turn right again into a less-traveled dirt track. This leads to the cliffs above Green Crater Lake. [Ask any Masai children or adults for directions, should you have problems locating the lake.]

☐ **Walk:** To reach the shore of Green Crater Lake, there are two safe options:
° Facing the water, walk to the right until you locate the easiest place to step down over the side of the cliff wall.
° Cycle to the opposite side of the lake where a footpath leads to the lakeshore. Women who do their washing in the lake enter by this footpath.

Backtrack along Moi Lake Rd. South to the exit point from Hell's Gate Park. Continue straight on Moi Lake Rd. South and follow the balance of the Easy Loop.

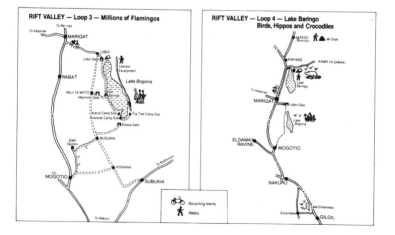

Rift Valley Loop 3
Millions Of Flamingos

Description: Lake Bogoria's western shore is the perfect place for quiet cycling while observing abundant bird and animal life. The lake's hot springs, reached after 8.5 miles (14 km), are much too hot for bathing. One wonders why flamingos enjoy such scalding waters. To test the water's temperatures, bring along some bananas and eggs to cook in the bubbling waters. The paved road ends not far beyond the hot springs, and a rocky dirt road leads to Acacia Campground (no water) and Fig Tree Camp, with its clear flowing stream. A rough track continues around the eastern shore which makes circling the lake possible for Hardcore and committed Challengers. A small admission fee is charged to enter Lake Bogoria Reserve and to camp.

Rating:	Easy	Challenger
Distance:	18 miles (30 km)	72 miles (120 km) return
Terrain:	Flat	Flat
Road Conditions:	Paved; low traffic	Paved, rocky dirt; low traffic.

Hardcore Option: 88 miles (146 km); Flat, hilly; Paved, rocky dirt, rough mountain trail; low traffic.

Walks:
- Hiking to the plateau of Laikipia Escarpment is an exhilarating workout.
- From Acacia Camp, walk along the shoreline trail towards Fig Tree Camp and the eastern shore.

Accommodation and Meals:
- Lake Bogoria Lodge recently opened 0.6 miles (1 km) from the Loboi Gate, on the paved road leading to Lake Bogoria (expensive rooms and restaurant).
- Camping is possible near Lake Bogoria's Park Gates, and at Acacia and Fig Tree Campgrounds on the south lakeshore
- Sodas and drinking water available at Loboi Gate, water at Fig Tree Camp. Camping is possible near the Park Gates, Acacia, and Fig Tree Campgrounds.

Starting point for Easy Option: Lake Bogoria Loboi Gate [Buses run frequently from Nakuru to Marigat. No buses travel from Marigat to Loboi Gate. If private transport and hitching are unavailable, cycle the 12 miles (20 km) on paved road from Marigat to Loboi Gate. Carry water.]

Follow the paved road beside the western lakeshore to the hot springs. Shade trees and spectacular vistas make picnicking at the hot springs a delight.

☐ **Sidetrip:** Continue cycling on the dirt track until a second series of hot springs are reached. Baboon families are generally in this vicinity.
Backtrack to the Loboi Gate.

☐ **Walks:** Leaving bikes at Loboi Gate, hike to Laikipia Escarpment plateau. An easier option is to visit nearby tribal villages on foot.

Starting Point of Challenger Option: Marigat trading center

Cycle south a short distance to the sign, Lake Bogoria, signaling a left turn to the Loboi Gate. Follow the Easy Option route to the hot springs. Continue on the dirt road cycling another 8.5 miles (14 km) to Fig Tree Campground. Greater Kudu and waterbuck are frequently seen in this area. Beware of the baboons at Fig Tree Camp: they steal.

☐ **Challenger Sidetrip or Walk:** Cycle or walk as far as time and energy allow on the Laikipia Escarpment track along the eastern lakeside. Backtrack to Fig Tree Camp, allowing enough time to arrive by 6:30 pm (Daylight hours are consistent on the equator year-round.)

Backtrack to Marigat. [South exits from this reserve are hilly and hot. Do not attempt them unless you have sufficient time and water.]

Starting Point for Hardcore Option: Marigat village. Follow the Challenger's route to Fig Tree Camp. Continue cycling on the track crossing the Laikipia Escarpment, skirting the eastern lakeside. [Bring clothing to protect arms and legs from thorn bushes.] Gametrackers Safari Company uses this tough route for its organized cycling safaris.

Backtrack to Marigat or camp near the Loboi Gate.

Rift Valley Loop 4
Lake Baringo: Birds, Hippos, and Crocodiles

Description: A gentle ride from Marigat brings cyclists to Lake Baringo's shore. Boat trips cruising the shoreline and beyond to the lake's islands are excellent bird and hippo watching outings. Walking to the small trading center of Kampi ya Samaki (*samaki* means fish in Swahili) is pleasant, but more informative are the morning and evening walks with Lake Baringo Club's resident ornithologist Hilary. This is an excellent way to start identifying many of the 500 resident species.

Hot, arid conditions north of Lake Baringo make cycling into this region strictly for strong cyclists who carry large water supplies. The stark isolation of the desolate Rift Valley floor is mysteriously attractive. If soaring temperatures can be tolerated, climbing to the crater rim of Silali Volcano (5008 feet, 1526 m) presents a genuine challenge.

Rating:	Easy	Challenger
Distance:	12 miles (20 km) each way	35–50 miles (60–80 km)
Terrain:	Flat	Flat, hilly

Road Conditions: Paved; low traffic / Paved; low traffic

Hardcore Option: 85–100 miles (140–165 km); Flat/hilly; Paved, dirt track; low traffic

Bringing home the fish on Rusinga Island, one of Lake Victoria's many islands. (photo Antonio Tliceto)

Sidetrips and Walks:
◦ Boat trips to Lake Baringo's islands followed by walks on the islands. Secluded camping is available
◦ Walks with Lake Baringo Club's resident ornithologist

Accommodation and Meals:
◦ Robert's Camp (budget *bandas*, camping; no restaurant)
◦ Lake Baringo Club Lodge (expensive rooms; restaurant and bar open to all, though a 50 shilling charge may be requested at the lodge gate for nonresidents of the hotel)
◦ Lake Baringo Island Safari Camp (expensive rooms; bar and restaurant)
◦ Basic food supplies are available in Kampi ya Samaki.

Starting point for Easy, Challenger, and Hardcore Options: Marigat. [Buses from Nakuru, Kabernet, or Eldoret travel here.]

Route Directions: Proceed north on B4 to the Baringo exit sign. Turn right. The entrance for Lake Baringo Club Lodge and Robert's Camp is one mile (2 km).

Either spend the night at Lake Baringo or backtrack to Marigat to end the tour.

☐ **Challenger and Hardcore Options:** return to B4 and turn right. Cycle north until the paved road ends.

☐ **Challenger Option:** Backtrack to Lake Baringo.

☐ **Hardcore Option:** Continue further north to Kinyang. Try to make arrangements here to climb Silali Volcano, including a local guide and vehicle support to carry additional water. When you feel confident that water supplies near Kapedo are sufficient, continue north of Kinyang, towards deserted Kapedo.

☐ **Walk:** To climb Silali Volcano, camping gear and all supplies including water must be carried.

☐ **Hardcore Option:** Backtrack to Lake Baringo.

CHAPTER 17

Western Kenya and Lake Victoria's Islands

Western Kenya slopes down to Lake Victoria separated from Central Kenya by the high Rift wall of the Mau and Elgeyo escarpments. Its diverse landscape contains dense farmlands, semi-desert, lush green hills, and still greener valleys. The eastern shoreline of Lake Victoria, Africa's largest lake and the world's third largest, also contributes to the spectacular contrasts western Kenya

offers. Steamers plying Lake Victoria make visits to islands and remote fishing villages convenient.

Young boys wash a mamba *near Homa Bay pier.*

Luo tribesmen farm the fertile land near Lake Victoria and fish its waters. When the Luo migrated to Western Kenya in the fifteenth century, they found untouched grasslands, thick forests, and abundant wildlife. Following cattle raids on other tribes, farming and fishing were adopted as major enterprises. Unlike many neighboring tribes, such as the Gusii, they do not circumcise. In former times children were initiated into adulthood by removing six teeth from the lower jaw. This tradition is rarely practiced today.

A renowned Luo in Kenya's history was Tom Mboya, a charismatic politician gunned to death in Nairobi in 1969. His death precipitated widespread rioting leading to forty-three deaths. On the north shore of Rusinga Island a mausoleum contains gifts and mementos of Mboya. A safari to Western Kenya from the Rift Valley town of Nakuru begins with a steep climb over Mau Summit. In Mau Forest live the few remaining Wanderobo tribesmen. They are extremely shy, diminutive honey-gatherers who dress in skins and are considered to be Kenya's oldest inhabitants.

Over the crest of Mau Summit lies a sea of vibrant green tea estates surrounding Kericho. At 6,000 feet (1,847 m) above sea level and blessed with equal amounts of rain and sunshine, Kericho follows only India and Sri Lanka in tea production. Several huge tea estates are open to visitors. Chagaik, an attractive estate located 4.8 miles (8 km) east of Kericho past the KETEPA compound, sports a lake and well-kept arboretum.

Kipsigis people living in Kericho are one of eight Kalenjin groups. The central feature of Kalenjin life is the initiation rite carried out after male circumcision and female clitoridectomy. During the various initiation stages, youths learn the rules of conduct and the prescribed penalties for those rules of adult society. Men may have several wives but not marry within clans. Most Kipsigis are agriculturists who grow millet and tend goat, sheep, or cattle.

South of Kericho beyond Sotik is Kisii town, the center of Gusii culture. This community bears the questionable honor of having the world's highest birthrate. Gusii inhabit much of the western highlands, though many were killed after resisting the British conquest in 1905. When World War I began, thousands of Gusii men were recruited by force into the despised Carrier Corps. Despite these brutalities, the tribe has maintained strong cultural traditions. Medicinemen remain important in their communities practicing trepanning. During this operation a small hole is placed in the skull to relieve headaches. It might even be a useful cure for cyclists' fatigue. Any takers?

While visiting in a Gusii home atop Manga Ridge, several interesting Gusii traditions surfaced. If a son marries, for example, the father can no longer enter into his son's home, though the son may visit both mother and father in the parents' home. Another tradition mandates that a son-in-law, when visiting his wife's relatives, may never eat eggs or chicken, though these items are served to other guests in his presence. Gusii practice male and female circumcision, which takes place between eight and 15 years.

Thirteen miles (22 km) south is Tabaka, Kenya's soapstone center. This picturesque hilltop village has large quarries of the soft pink and white stone. Villagers have become expert craftsmen carving this soapstone into chess sets, figurines, and vases for export to other parts of Kenya and the world.

Lake Victoria's fascinations are many. A word of caution: avoid swimming in the lake due to the dangers of bilharzia.

In the hills above Kisii, professional sitting under trees carve soapstone taken from the Tabaka Caverns.

Instead, enjoy the coastline which has a host of small fishing villages to explore. Ferries carry passengers to Rusinga and Mfangano Islands, and between Homa Bay, Kendu Bay, and Kisumu.

Like Nairobi, Kisumu owes its growth to the Uganda Railway which reached there in 1901. For many years after, this major port boasted customs and immigration facilities. Port activity has largely died out, but Kisumu remains Kenya's third largest city.

Wildlife is not so plentiful in Western Kenya as elsewhere, but Ruma National Park offers fine game-viewing without tourist crowds. Jackson's Hartebeest, rare Roan and Oribi antelopes, and Rothchild's giraffe live within the park. Cycle to the Park (see *Western Kenya Loop 5*, this chapter) or arrange for transport through the Homa Bay Hotel.

Grand Tour
Western Kenya And Lake Victoria's Islands

Starting Point for Challenger and Easy Options: Kisumu [Kenya's famous railway, the 'Lunatic Express,' travels to Kisumu from Nairobi every evening. Sleeping compartments and dining cars make this inexpensive journey a comfortable experience. Bus service to Kericho or Kisumu is also available from Nairobi, Nakuru, and points in between.]

Starting Point for Hardcore Option: Nakuru, continuing west over the steep Mau Summit. [For cycling directions from Nairobi to Nakuru, see *Grand Tour: Rift Valley Wonders*.]

Hardcore Route Directions: Cycle west on A104 from Nakuru. Two options for crossing the Mau Summit exist:
- After four miles (7 km), turn left towards Njoro on C56. Njoro Valley is a major cheese-producing area. After 33 miles (55 km), passing Njoro and Elburgon, is Molo. Either turn right on D318 five miles (8km) to rejoin A104 or continue straight through Molo to connect with B1, the highway to Kericho; or
- Stay on A104 reaching Mau Summit after 30 miles (51 km). Generally A104 has low traffic and a good paved surface. Turn left on B1 towards Kericho, another 25 miles (42 km) southwest.

☐ **Sidetrip:** At the toll booth on B1, locate a right turn to Londiani on C35, passing Kipkelion to rejoin B1 further west after 12 miles (20 km). Visit Lumbwa Monastery in

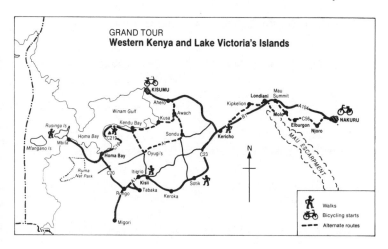

Kipkelion, a Trappist monk community. 13 miles (22 km) after rejoining B1, Kericho is reached.

Watch for the speed bumps when approaching Kericho. There are many! The charming old Tea Hotel is 1 mile (2 km) ahead on the left. Spend the night or at least stop for tea to see this relic of Kenya's colonial past. Further on is the moderately priced Mid-west Hotel. The New Tas and Tas Motels offer budget lodging.

☐ **Challenger Option:** If you have have arrived in Kisumu by train, you can join the Grand Tour at Kericho by cycling southwest on B1 from Kisumu for 33 miles (56 km).

☐ **Sidetrip and Walk:** See Western Kenya — Loop 1, below, for a tour of Chagaik Tea Estate

Leave Kericho cycling south on C23. After 24 miles (40 km) Sotik is reached. Sotik's trading center is .25 miles (.5 km) off the highway. Note the contrast between the contemporary Barclays Bank building and Sotik's other simple structures.

☐ **Walk:** Pass through Sotik trading center to the Catholic Diocese compound. Beyond this compound are many walking trails leading into green valleys. Kipsigis people living in this area are extremely friendly. From Sotik, B1 is overhung with trees. Openings through the trees provide long views across the hillside shambas. Excellent road surface continues.

After 15 miles (25 km) Keroka trading center is reached. Meals and accommodation is limited to basic establishments. In another 15 miles (25 km) is Kisii.

Upon Entering Kisii the Mwalimu Hotel is on the right (moderate rooms and dining). Continue through Kisii town center to Kisii Hotel, an older hostelry with lovely gardens, budget rooms, and restaurant. Safe Lodge in the town center is a favorite with budget travelers.

☐ **Sidetrip and Walk:** Cycle or walk to the edge of Kissi (direction Kericho). Passing the Sports Club, turn left into a dirt track. Continue 3.3 miles (5.5 km) to an unmarked road on the left. Cross the bridge and in three miles (6 km) a small settlement is reached. Leave bikes with a woman or *mzee* (older person) and start the 20-minute walk to the Manga Ridge summit. Continue left along the edge of the Ridge to visit St. Paul's Polytechnic School, a mud-brick structure where dressmaking and carpentry are taught using basic equipment. From St. Paul's, follow the lower trail back to the village, passing traditional Gusii homes on the right. Gusiis are extremely hospitable and friendly people. By asking, camping anywhere in this highland haven is surely possible. Backtrack to Kisii.

Leave Kisii via the route outlined in *Western Kenya Loop 2*, this chapter.

☐ **Sidetrip and Walk:** Visit the soapstone carvers of Tabaka village. Refer to *Western Kenya Loop 2*. From Kisii to Rongo is 14 miles (23 km). Turn right at Rongo towards Homa Bay on C20. This stretch is flat and paved with low traffic. Homa Bay is reached after 19 miles (32 km).

☐ **Walks:** Homa Bay has two prominent conical-shaped hills that can be climbed.

° The taller is Got Asego. From Homa Bay Hotel, walk through the trading center, passing the Total gas station, to the second left. Beyond Homa Bay High School turn right for 0.5 miles (0.8 km). After the Water Works and

It is highly unlikely that you will glimpse a lion or any other similar predator outside the national parks. This lion was photographed in the Masai Mara Reserve, where cyclists and walkers are not allowed.

Forest Department on the right, follow the trail to the summit for a 360-degree view of Lake Victoria and surrounding areas.

° To climb the lower conical hill, Kasarwa, walk to the lakefront near the pier. Keep right following the shoreline until reaching the base of Kasarwa.

☐ **Sidetrip:** From Homa Bay, ferries sail to Mbita–Rusinga Island (daily) and Mfangano Island (twice weekly — probably on Friday and Tuesday, though schedules change). Fishing boats carry passengers to Mfangano from Mbita and Rusinga Island. Bicycles are welcome aboard.

☐ **More Sidetrips and Walks:** from Rusinga Island. See *Western Kenya Loop 4*, this chapter.

Leaving Homa Bay, cycle north on C19, a gravel road.

☐ **Sidetrip and Walk:** Turn left when you reach the sign *Homa Hills Centre*. This dirt road skirts the lakeshore. Homa Mountain is a challenging walk that takes about three hours, with a short rock scramble near the summit. Check *Western Kenya Loop 3*, this chapter, for the details. Kendu Bay is reached after 19 miles (32 km).

From Kendu Bay, select one of these two options:
° Cycle on the dirt road inland to Oyugis. Continue north on A1 to Sondu, Awach, Ahero, and Kisumu; or
° Continue north on C19 to Kusa, Awach, and Kisumu.

From Kisumu: Kakamega Forest lies 30 miles (50 km) north of Kisumu, easily accessed from the Northwest or Western Grand Tours. Do not miss it. See *Northwest Kenya and the Cherangani Hills Loop 4*, in Chapter 18.

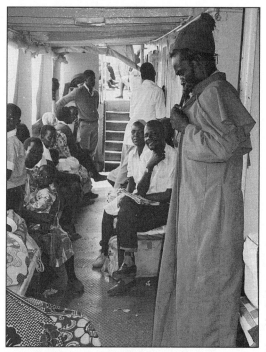

Aboard a steamer on Lake Victoria ferrying passengers from Homa Bay to Mbita-Rusinga Island.

Western Kenya Loop 1
More Tea, Please: Kericho's Tea Estates and Arboretum

Description: Kericho is Kenya's 'tea capital,' and cycling through a tea estate is the best way to learn how tea is grown and harvested. Endless rows of vibrant green tea bushes stretch over gently rolling hills surrounding Kericho. An arboretum, started by an Englishman who once managed Chagaik Estate, creates a lovely park for picnicking. Occupying one bank of a stream flowing into a fishing lake, the arboretum is visited by monkeys and birds, though many more are seen on the opposite bank darting in and out of tangled, tropical trees.

Rating: Easy

Distance: 10–12 miles (16—0 km)

Terrain: Flat

Road Conditions: Paved, dirt roads on the estate; moderate to low traffic

Sidetrip and Walks:

157

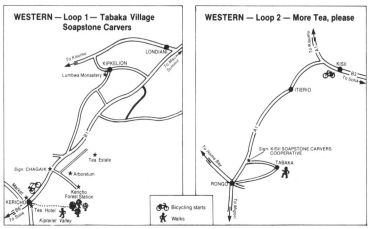

- Cycle to Kericho Forest Station
- Walk through the Chagaik Arboretum and Tea Estate

Accommodation and Meals:
- Tea Hotel (expensive rooms and restaurant)
- Mid-West Hotel (moderate rooms and restaurant)
- New Tas and Tas Motels (budget rooms and restaurant)
- Take a picnic lunch to Chagaik Estate

Starting Point: Tea Hotel in Kericho

Route Directions: Cycle east on B1 (direction Mau Summit) 4.5 miles (7.5 km). Turn right at the sign *Chagaik*, and immediately turn left to the Arboretum on the stream bank. Straight ahead is a shelter where tea pickers take tea breaks (which seems immensely appropriate). Visiting the tea pickers is fun, and they seem to enjoy guests during break times.

☐ **Walk**: On foot visit the arboretum, lake, and tea fields to observe how tea is picked, leaf-by-leaf, and briskly tossed over one shoulder into a large round basket strapped to the picker's back. [Before entering tea fields where men are working, locate a supervisor and ask for permission to enter or to photograph anyone.]

☐ **Sidetrip:** Backtrack to the road connecting B1 with the estate. Turn left, cycling 2.5 miles (4.5 km) to Kericho Forest Station.

Backtrack to the Tea Hotel. Relax, enjoy a cup of tea or something stronger from the Tea Hotel bar. You have earned it!

Western Kenya Loop 2
Tabaka Soapstone Carvers

Description: In the Kisii hills is a small village where a bustling soapstone trade has developed. From Tabaka's quarries huge blocks of creamy white, pink, and beige soapstone are taken for locally manufactured handicrafts. Skilled carvers specialize in making certain items. One man may carve only elephants, another only chessboards. Only men are carvers, as you will observe. These 'professionals' are found sitting under trees and on verandas of small houses with rough chunks of soapstone awaiting the artist's touch. The large Soapstone Carvers Cooperative Building displays the wares of local craftsmen. Wooden three-legged stools with intricately inset bead patterns are also carved here.

Rating: Challenger

Distance: 34 miles (56 km)

Terrain: Hilly

Road Conditions: Paved, dirt; low traffic

Sidetrip and Walks: Walk to the quarries, through Tabaka village and into the forest or cycle to Homa Bay.

Accommodation and Meals:
- Tabaka has no lodges; use *hotelis* for dining. Basic fruits, vegetables, bread, sodas, and *chai* (tea) are available in Tabaka and Rongo.

Starting Point: Kisii

Route Directions: Leave Kisii on A1, direction Migori. After 4.2 miles (7 km), Itierio is reached. In my memory, this is the 'banana village,' remembered for the large bunches of bananas that hang from every roadside *dulca*.

Continue 5.5 miles (9 km) to the sign *Kisii Soap Carvers Cooperative*. Turn left; the dirt road becomes hilly before reaching Tabaka.

After 3 miles (5 km) soapstone shops begin to appear. A large Cooperative store is .5 miles (1 km) further.

☐ **Walk:** Leave bikes at the Cooperative Shop. Exiting the compound gate, turn left to the corner, then right. Continue straight to reach a soapstone quarry. En route many *jua kali* (hot sun) workers are practicing their crafts. Turn left into the quarry. (Remember to ask before photographing anyone. Several workers refused permission to me.) Backtrack to the Cooperative gate. Walk straight towards the Mission Hospital. At the Mission, turn left into the trading center. When the street ends, turn right for a forest walk.

When leaving Tabaka, two options are offered. The second is more difficult:

° Backtrack to A1, or
° Cycle past the quarry, visited during the Walk, along the rough dirt road for 6 miles (10 km), joining A1.

Either turn right, backtracking to Kisii, or turn left to Rongo.

☐ **Sidetrip:** From Rongo, cycle west to Homa Bay and Lake Victoria. See Western Kenya and Lake Victoria's Islands Grand Tour: Rongo to Homa Bay.

Near Kenya's tea capital Kericho, tea pickers on the Chagaik Estate enjoy meeting cyclists and walkers during their tea break.

Western Kenya Loop 3
Mysterious Lake and Pottery Makers:
Kendu Bay and Homa Mountain

Description: Sailing on Lake Victoria, exploring Luo fishing villages, visiting the workshops of pottery makers and weavers, climbing the Western Coast's highest mountain, and solving the riddle of a mysterious lake are the chief attractions of this tour. Undoubtedly, you will discover many more. By taking the ferry from Kisumu to Kendu Bay, and possibly onwards to Homa Bay, Lake Victoria's Coast is explored in a relaxed way.

At the small port of Kendu Bay, a walk to the mysterious Simbi Lake should not be missed. Though this circular lake rests only a short distance from Lake Victoria, it has no apparent source. A Luo legend relates that one night an old woman was denied fire at the village once occupying the present lake site. She left that place accompanied by a young woman who had offered to help her. Later that night rain poured, swamping the village. Thus, the legend goes, Simbi Lake was formed, and the village disappeared forever.

Opposite the dirt road to Simbi Lake is a sign, Kanyadhiang Awagh Handkraft, pointing toward a unique handicraft enterprise. In the Spinner's Hall Luo women spin and weave local designs into tablecloths, pillow covers, shirts, and rugs.

161

Oriang Pottery Centre is 1.3 miles (2 km) further south on the Homa Bay Rd. Watch for the dirt road on the left; no signs mark this corner. This centre was started as a United Nations-

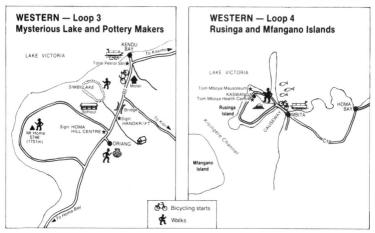

sponsored venture to train local women in the art of pottery making. Oriang receives orders from hotels, restaurants, and individuals for pottery lamp bases, candle holders, mugs, and even statuary.

Dominating the Coast between Homa Bay and Kendu Bay is Homa Mountain. The three-hour round trip walk to its summit is highly recommended. A trail, found on the mountain's western side near Homa Hills Centre, climbs through thick bush where monkeys frolic. Ask for a guide at the Polytechnic School near Homa Hills Centre and offer to pay for this service. You could eventually find the trail on your own, but most of the fascination of being out in the bush in Africa is getting to know the people.

Rating: Easy

Distance: 19 miles (32 km)

Terrain: Flat

Road Conditions: Dirt; low traffic

Sidetrips and Walks:
◦   Walk the trail encircling Simbi Lake
◦   Walk through Oriang to the river clay beds
◦   Cycle the coastal road circling the peninsula to Homa
◦   Hills Centre

- Hike to the summit of Homa Mountain

Accommodation and Meals:
- Kendu Bay: Nipe Nikupe Motel (budget rooms only). New and tricky to find. Take the road opposite the Total Station traveling away from the lake. The first right leads to this quiet inn. Mary Okoth and her husband, the owners, display genuine Luo hospitality.
- Kendu Bay: The Diner behind the Total Station is a short walk from Nipe Nikupe (meaning 'hand in hand' in Luo)
- Homa Bay: Homa Bay Hotel (moderate rooms and restaurant on Lake Victoria's shore)
- Masawa Hotel (budget rooms and restaurant)
- Homa Mountain: Camping only. Ask at the Homa Hills Health Centre for assistance in locating a safe site.

Starting Point: Kendu Bay [Reach Kendu Bay from Kisumu by ferry or cycling.]

Route Directions: From Kendu Bay Port, cycle to B2 highway; continue south passing the Kisii turning on the left.

After 2.5 miles (4 km) a river bridge is crossed. Turn right on a minor dirt road to Simbi Lake.

☐ **Walk:** A trail encircles Simbi Lake. Flamingos and other water birds nest along the shore. Visit the primary school on the hill overlooking the lake.

Backtrack to B2. Cross to the opposite side where a sign, Kanyadhiang Awagh Handkraft, marks the road to the Spinner's Hall. After visiting Spinner's Hall, Backtrack to B2. Cycle south, towards Homa Bay. After 1 mile (2 km) turn left on a dirt road to Oriang. This turning is not signposted.

☐ **Walk:** After visiting Oriang Pottery Centre, ask a local for directions to the riverbed where clay for the pottery is extracted. Yield to the temptation to get your hands into the clay and mold something more strange than marvelous.

From Oriang, backtrack to B2. You can turn right or left on B2. A right turn leads in 1.3 miles (2 km) to a sign, Homa Hills Centre. A right turn at this sign allows you to take the sidetrip to climb Homa Mountain and cycle the peninsula. By continuing straight on B2, you will arrive quickly in

Kendu Bay. If turning left on B2 from Oriang, you will reach Homa Bay in 19 miles (32 km).

☐ **Sidetrip and Walk:** Turn left at the sign, Homa Hills Centre, and follow this road 13 miles (22 km). At the Centre or nearby Polytechnic School inquire for a local guide to climb Homa Mountain. If 'Churchill' is still around, he is an excellent guide. After the three-hour return walk to Homa Mountain, continue cycling on the road circling this peninsula. After 14 miles (24 km), B2 is rejoined. Either return to Kendu Bay and take the ferry to Homa Bay, Mbita-Rusinga Island or Kisumu, or cycle south to Homa Bay, a 19 mile (32 km) ride.

Western Kenya Loop 4
Rusinga and Mfangano Islands

Description: Island hopping in Lake Victoria while visiting dozens of Luo fishing villages is easy to do. Ferries connect Kisumu, Kendu Bay, Homa Bay, Mbita-Rusinga Island, and Mfangano Island. Small fishing boats can take you where the large ferries cannot. Sailing to small, remote islands where few or no tourists have ever set foot is a real African adventure. Put Conrad's *Heart of Darkness* out of mind. Such stories have tainted too many thoughts about Africa. Luos, one of Kenya's largest tribes, are delightfully friendly. Most likely someone will invite you for dinner, an experience I encourage you not to miss. (Show up with plenty of extra food and treats bought from village *dukas*; these people are desperately poor though they will ask for nothing.)

From the village of Mbita, a short causeway connects the mainland to Rusinga Island. A dirt road circling the island and footpaths crisscrossing it are perfect for cycling and walking. Traffic consists of three or four *matatu* pick-ups which occasionally clamor down the road. Rusinga's attractions are Tom Mboya's Mausoleum (his parents died in 1989 and 1990, though several brothers remain on the family plot), wide open spaces, and friendly Luo people.

These mambas *are used to transport many of the country's rural goods, such as these bundles of sisal, to market.*

Spend an unusual and thoroughly exciting evening with Luos while Omena fishing. Paddling out into Lake Victoria's dark waters, fishermen set floating lanterns beside their boats to attract tiny Omena fish into their nets. You will be surprised at the number of lanterns glowing in the lake's waters. Mfangano Island has no cars and few bicycles, but plenty of walking paths. Local guides know the site of old rock paintings. To reach Mfangano, take one of the twice-weekly steamers from Homa Bay making stops at Mbita and Mfangano. These steamers depart Homa Bay at 2:15 pm sharp (I know. I arrived at 2:18 pm to watch the ferry sail away). If the steamer schedule to Mfangano does not fit your plans, locate the brightly painted fishing canoes on Mbita's shores any morning and ask for a lift to Mfangano.

Rating: Easy

Distance: 10 miles (16 km)

Terrain: Flat

Road Conditions: Dirt tracks; no traffic

Sidetrip and Walks:
° Loop 4 may be walked or cycled.

A catch of Nile perch and tilapia are being weighed on the shores of Rusinga Island.

- Many small islands are scattered throughout Lake Victoria's waters; most are inhabited by small clans of Luos. Arrange with a canoe 'captain' to carry you to islands rarely visited by foreigners. Bring camping equipment and food supplies, since Lake Victoria's occasionally turbulent waters may delay the return.
- Walk to Tom Mboya's Mausoleum
- Omena fishing
- Walk across Mfangano Island to see rock paintings

Accommodation and Meals:
- Mbita: Safari Lodge is new and definitely the top choice (budget rooms); *hotelis* for dining.
- Rusinga Island: has a small *hoteli* near the Tom Mboya Medical Centre
- Mfangano Island: zilch! Bring camping and food supplies

Starting Point: Mbita [reached from Homa Bay, Kendu Bay, or Kisumu by ferry]

Route Directions: From Mbita Port, cycle across the causeway. Stay on the only main road circling the island until reaching Kaswanga.

☐ **Walk:** If you prefer walking and climbing the rocky bluffs over cycling around Rusinga, follow the trails heading north, keeping to the right of the large bluff. After one hour (or less) the tiny settlement of Kaswanga is reached. Some of the tastiest and most appreciated *chapatis* (flat bread) in Kenya are served at the Kaswanga *hoteli*. While taking refreshments, play a game of checkers using bottle caps and a homemade board with one of the locals.

Continue another mile (2 km) to Tom Mboya's Mausoleum. En route, near the lakeshore but well concealed, is a posh sportsfishing camp for tourists flown to Rusinga from Masai Mara Reserve.

Leaving the Mausoleum, walk or cycle to the fishing village directly ahead near the lakeshore where huge nets filled with Omena cover the ground.

Follow the road (the one-and-only road) back to Mbita. Return to Homa Bay on the daily ferry departing Mbita at 8:15 am or cycle to Homa Bay if the roads are dry.

Western Kenya Loop 5
Homa Bay to Ruma National Park

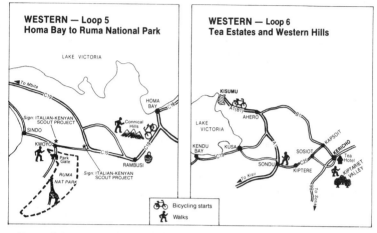

Description: Ruma National Park is reached via a backroad branching off the main Homa Bay-Mbita road. Scenic delights along the way are distinctive clusters of conical hills above sweeping valleys and small Luo settlements with markets.

Ruma National Park does not officially allow walkers or cyclists within the park (a policy difficult to believe when observing many locals cycling and walking along the main park road). The park's wildlife consists primarily of Roan antelope, kongoni, and giraffe, so potential dangers to travelers outside motor vehicles seem small. Unless visitors can convince Rangers that they, like the locals, need to cross the park to the community on the other side, they may be stopped at the Park Gate. If this happens, consider a foot safari into the Park accompanied by a Ranger-guide. Whether entering through the gate or not, cycling to Ruma National Park is scenically worthwhile and you are likely to see Roan antelope and oribi anyway.

Rating: Challenger

Distance: 36 miles (60 km)

Terrain: Hilly

Road Conditions: Graded dirt; low traffic

Walk: Walk into the cluster of conical hills and through Luo villages. Villages offer markets on different weekdays; inquire in local villages for market dates.

Accommodation and Meals:
- Homa Bay: Homa Bay Hotel (moderate rooms and restaurant) on Lake Victoria's shore
- Masawa Hotel (budget rooms and restaurant)
- Ruma National Park: campsites with no facilities

Starting Point: Homa Bay

Route Directions: Leave Homa Bay on the dirt road to Mbita. After 8 miles (13 km), conical hills are on the right.

☐ **Walk:** This large cluster of conical hills offers fine walking possibilities. Allow at least several hours to venture into these hills.

From Homa Bay, it is 10 miles (16 km) to the yellow sign, Italian-Kenyan Scout Project. [No sign for Ruma National Park appears until the park gate.] Turn left.

Continue 6.5 miles (11 km) until another yellow sign appears like the first. At the second yellow sign turn sharply left to the road approaching Ruma National Park Gate.

☐ **Walk:** A foot safari into Ruma National Park is a superb way to see the wildlife (Review the section *Using Guides* in Chapter 8, *Getting Along with the Locals*). Negotiate this option with Park Rangers and offer to pay for guide services.

Backtrack to the Mbita road. Options:
- Turn right to return to Homa Bay, or
- Turn left to cycle 15 miles (25 km) to Mbita. For Mbita and Rusinga Island tours, see *Western Kenya Loop 4*.

Western Kenya Loop 6
Tea Estates and Western Hills, Kisumu, and the Interior

Description: A walking tour of Kisumu takes in the port, market, (baskets, pots, Luo kitchenware), and the informative Kisumu Museum (look for the unusual Luo 'harps' at the Museum Gift Shop). Strolling through the Impala Park Orphanage (adjacent to the Sunset Hotel) is conveniently combined with a short cycling trip to Dunga fishing village. It is sad to see animals caged, but the impala and monkeys roam freely and park rangers are well informed on the district's wildlife. Hippo Point, Dunga Restaurant, and Camp are directly ahead. Follow the signs.

Leaving Lake Victoria's blue waters and traveling inland, cyclists ride through lush country adorned with green hills and extensive tea estates. This circular route explores the interior south and east of Kisumu. At Sondu, reached from Kisumu via A1 south, a Catholic mission crafts miniature terra cotta figures. A dirt track from Sondu cuts east 15 miles (25 km) to the "tea capital" of Kenya, Kericho (See Western Kenya — Loop 1). Return to Kisumu by bus or cycle the B1 highway which carries moderate traffic.

Rating:	Challenger	Hardcore
Distance:	50 miles (80 km) to Kericho	93 miles (155 km) to Kisumu
Terrain:	Hilly	Hilly

Road Conditions: Paved, dirt; low traffic

Sidetrips and Walks:
° See *Western Kenya Loop 1*, above, for walks and sidetrips from Kericho. Walk through the Kiptariet Valley and Kericho Forest behind Kericho's Tea Hotel
° From Sondu, cycle to Kusa on Lake Victoria's coast.

Accommodation and Meals:
° Kisumu: Imperial Hotel (moderate rooms and restaurant)
° Sunset Hotel (expensive rooms and restaurant)
° Dunga Camp (camping and budget restaurant) Kericho-Tea Hotel (expensive rooms and moderate restaurant)
° Mid-West Hotel (moderate rooms and restaurant)
° New Tas and Tas Motels (budget rooms and restaurant)

Starting Point: Kisumu

Route Directions: Cycle south on the A1 — B1 highway towards Ahero.

At Ahero, visit the heronry which also attracts storks, ibis, cormorant, and egrets.

From Ahero, ride south to Sondu and visit the Catholic mission.

☐ **Sidetrip:** From Sondu, cycle the dirt road west to Kusa on Lake Victoria's Coast, joining the coastal road leading north to Kisumu and south to Kendu Bay.

Leave Sondu via the backroad which joins B1 north of Kericho. Turn right on B1 and cycle south to Kericho.

☐ **Walk:** Walk into the lovely Kiptariet Valley behind the Tea Hotel. Cross a footbridge leading into Kericho Forest.

See *Western Kenya Loop 1*, above, for more Sidetrips and Walks.

☐ **Challenger Option:** Stay overnight in Kericho or return to Kisumu by bus.

☐ **Hardcore Option:** Cycle to Kisumu via B1 West.

CHAPTER 18

Northwest Kenya and the Cherangani Hills

Northwest Kenya's landscape is dominated by dramatic and sometimes impenetrable mountain ranges dropping into broad valleys. The Cherangani Hills, rising to 12,000 feet (3,700 m), form the western wall of the Rift Valley's Elgeyo Escarpment which plummets 5,000 feet (1,500 m) into the Kerio Valley. At the base of the Cheranganis, northwestern deserts stretch into infinity.

Within these hills are forests and some of the finest mountain landscapes in Kenya. Best of all, it is possible to travel for days through this lush region, from one picturesque village to the next, without ever seeing other tourists.

The weeks I have trekked in the Cheranganis form my most precious memories of Kenya. Hopefully your experiences in these hills will be similarly rewarding. This mountainous region is captivating for many reasons. Colorful Pokot people, building distinctive round houses and observing ancient traditions, certainly enhance the pleasures of travel here. Belonging to the Kalenjin group, this tribe has always had nomadic clans. Most Pokots are pastorialists, however, and the remaining are cattle herders. Until recently, Pokot looked upon an individual who attended school as one lost to his tribe. This attitude is slowly changing.

Not all Pokot circumcise. For those who do, circumcision takes place between the ages of 15–20 years for boys and after age 12 for girls. After two or three months of seclusion, a public celebration introduces the participants as new adults. Boys start owning animals and may be sent to raid cows from other ethnic groups. Men marry numerous wives if they demonstrate sufficient wealth to the brides' parents.

West of the Cheranganis is the second highest mountain in Kenya, Mt. Elgon. This extinct volcano's 60-mile (100 km) base offers a panoply of hiking and cycling trails. Elgon was formed 8–10 million years ago and has not erupted for at least three million years. A five-mile (8 km) wide caldera has hot springs suitable for bathing. Higher up are caves once occupied by El Kony Masai. Colonial rulers forced these Masai from the caves, insisting they live in the open to be counted easily. These days elephants pay frequent visits to the caves mining for salt.

To the south are the Nandi Hills, inhabited by another Kalenjin tribe, where wild and bleak scrublands mingle with fertile sugar and tea estates. Nandi people are fiercely independent. They resisted interchange with foreigners for many years, and their warriors were reported to be brutal and daring, a reputation reinforced by frequent cattle raids on the Masai. Between 1895 and 1905, Nandi openly opposed the British by sabotaging the railroad's progress (stealing copper telegraph wires for jewelry making), and raiding cattle wherever possible. In retaliation, more than 1,000 Nandi warriors were killed by the British during this period. The tribe's spiritual leader, Koitalel, after agreeing to a truce, was killed by the British anyway. Nandi were forced into a reserve, and their lands were given to settlers.

Pokot tribesman in the unspoiled and scenically spectacular Cherangani Hills.

Northwest Kenya includes the Kakamega rain forest with its profuse variety of birds, monkeys, and other animal species surviving nowhere else in East Africa. Kakamega town, founded as a trading center along an ox-trail once leading to the Coast, is largely inhabited by the Luyia tribe.

Saiwa Swamp National Park allows visitors to climb into treehouses to observe the shy Sitatunga antelopes and a wide variety of water birds. If you value mountain scenery, glorious, quiet walks, and look forward to meeting some of Kenya's least acculturated people — *Karibuni!* Welcome to Northwest Kenya.

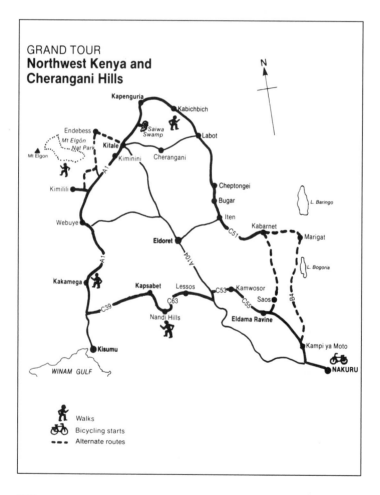

Grand Tour: Northwest Kenya and Cherangani Hills

Accommodation and Meals:
- Kapernet: Kabarnet Hotel, Box 42013, Nairobi. Tel. 29751, 23488. (moderate rooms and restaurant)
- Basic lodges and *hotelis* are sprinkled throughout the Hills.
- Camping is possible almost anywhere, but first ask the Chief for permission (see the section, *Protocol: Meeting the Chief* in Chapter 8, *Getting Along with the Locals*).

Starting point: Nakuru. [Nakuru is reached by bus from Nairobi, Naivasha, Eldoret, Kisumu, and many towns. For cycling directions to Nakuru from Nairobi, refer to the *Rift Valley Grand Tour*].

Route Directions: Two routes for leaving Nakuru are suggested, though the first is strictly for Hardcore cyclists. It is probably the toughest ride in Kenya.

☐ **Option a:** Leave Nakuru cycling north on B4 to Marigat. From Marigat, turn left to climb a steep winding road 18 miles (30 km) to Kabarnet. Spectacular if somewhat hair-raising vistas over Lake Baringo and the Rift Valley gradually appear.

☐ **Option b:** Leave Nakuru cycling north on B4. After 12 miles (20 km), at Kampi ya Moto, (Swahili, for 'Hot Camp') turn left towards Eldama Ravine, a sprawling trading center which occupies both sides of a steep gorge, reached in 22 miles (37 km). 4 miles (7 km) before Eldama Ravine, turn north to Saos and, in 42 miles (70 km), reach Kabarnet.

From Kabarnet head west on C51 to Iten, a 30-mile (50 km) ride.

At Iten, leave C51 and cycle north on the thrilling, though inappropriately named, Cherangani Highway. Actually this road is nothing more than a dirt track, albeit a well-maintained one, though conditions worsen in wet seasons. Check with local *matatu* drivers if the road condition is doubtful.

Walks: Days or weeks can be spent hiking and cycling in the Cherangani Hills. You will often be tempted to deviate from the direct route. A seemingly inexhaustible number of mountains await trekkers, with Chemnirot and Maral being the

175

highest. Komelogan, Kalelaigelat (referred to locally as 'white teeth' because of its white rock outcroppings), Koh in the north, and Kabichbich near the town of the same name offer spectacular mountain scenery. Ask Pokots to be guides. It is their land; they know the best trails and water sources. From Iten to Kapenguria it is 72 miles (120 km) passing through Bugar, Cheptongei, Labot, and Kabichbich trading centers.

From Kapenguria, take A1 south eight miles (13 km) to a delightful walking or resting base, Sirikwa Safari Guesthouse and Camp. Cycle south six miles (10 km) to Saiwa Swamp National Park (see *Northwest Kenya Loop 2*, below, for details).

Continue south on A1 10 miles (16 km) to Kitale (see *Western Kenya Loop 3*, below, to tour Mt. Elgon's crater and forests).

Follow A1 south of Kitale 60 miles (100 km) to Kakamega and the rain forest (see *Northwest Kenya Loop 4*, below, for accommodation in Kakamega and a forest tour). Don't miss cycling to the Forest Rest House within Kakamega Forest where camping and rooms are available.

Pokot and Marakwet peoples paint their picturesque round houses with broad salmon, black, and white stripes.

Leave Kakamega town traveling south on A1 10 miles (16 km) until reaching the turnoff east to Kapsabet (see *Western Kenya Loop 5* in Chapter 17).

From Kapsabet cycle south to the trading center, Nandi Hills (follow *Western Kenya Loop 5* as far as Nandi Hills).

☐ **Walk:** Nandi Hills is the haunt of the mysterious Nandi Bear, and a sighting of this elusive creature could make you instantly famous… See *Western Kenya Loop 5* in Chapter 17 for walking suggestions. [Hint: The best way to secure guides and cooperation for walks in rural country is to stress that you find the region very attractive. Say that you want to spend more time there and walk into the more remote areas. This removes any suspicions that you might have less altruistic reasons for visiting the hills]. Leave Nandi Hills trading center on C63 west passing through Lessos to join A104. Cycle north on A104 a short distance before connecting with C53.

Follow C53 to Kamwosor. Keep south on C55 to Eldama Ravine. Backtrack to Kampi ya Moto. (Follow the second option, starting this Grand Tour in reverse to reach Nakuru.) From Kampi ya Moto a short ride south on B4 ends this Grand Tour at Nakuru.

Northwest Kenya Loop 1
Cherangani Hills, Mountain Walking Extraordinaire

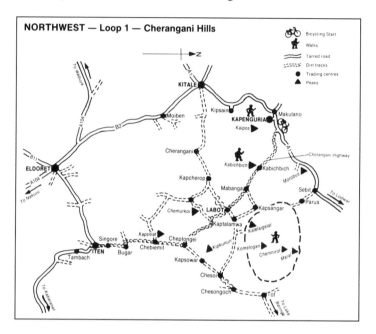

Description: For intrepid cyclists who do not have the time to ride the entire Cherangani Highway from Iten to Kapenguria, this loop presents the challenge and beauty of Kenya's Cherangani Hills. Kapenguria's historical import stems from the rigged trial of Jomo Kenyatta in the 1950s held by the colonial government. As expected, he was convicted on fabricated evidence and sentenced to prison for seven years. The schoolroom in Kapenguria where the trial took place and Kenyatta's prison cell are national monuments. Since the Cheranganis offer some extraordinarily grand walking trails (with the bonus of superb birdwatching), stay at least several days and use Kabichbich or Kapsangar as a base.

Rating: Hardcore [To adapt this tour to Easy or Challenger rating, catch a *matatu* to Kabichbich from Makutano. Guides for Cherangani foot safaris, lasting several hours or days, are available through Sirikwa Safari Guesthouse and Camp, 12 miles (20 km) north of Kitale. No phone. Write Jane Barnley, Box 332, Kitali, Kenya, to reserve guides.]

Distance: 50 miles (83 km)

Terrain: Mountainous

Road Conditions: Paved, dirt; low traffic

Sidetrips: Gentle walks or steep climbs into the hills

Accommodation and Meals:
- North of Kitale: Sirikwa Safari Guesthouse and Camp (moderate rooms, camping and dining for guests)
- Saiwa Swamp National Park: camping, no food
- Cherangani Hills: Scattered lodges, *hotelis*, camping practically everywhere
- West of Kitale: Mt. Elgon Lodge (moderate rooms and restaurant)

Starting Point: Kapenguria

Route Directions: Cycle north three miles (5 km) to Makutano. Turn east on the Cherangani Highway reaching Kabichbich after 20 miles (35 km). This road is steep! Stop often to look behind for stunning views of Mt. Elgon in the western horizon.

☐ **Walks:** Arrange to store bikes through the Chief in Kabichbich. From Kabichbich take a short and not difficult walk to the summit of Kabichbich Mountain; or take a one-hour (each way) walk to Kapsangar. Avoid the road and stick to mountain trails passing through Pokot villages and farms.

From Kabichbich, cycle east on the Cherangani Highway 12 miles (20 km) to Lobot. Turn south nine miles (15 km) to Kapcherop. A well-maintained road from Kapcherop leads directly west to Kitale.

From Kitale ride north to the Sirikwa Safari Guesthouse and Camp, west to Endebess and the Mt. Elgon Lodge, or choose from several lodges in Kitale.

Northwest Kenya Loop 2
Saiwa Swamp National Park

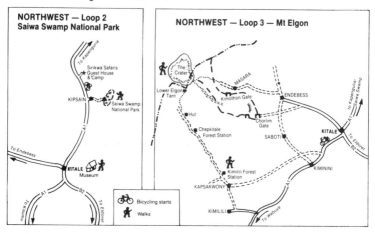

Description: Saiwa Swamp, near the Cherangani Hills, is situated at an altitude of 6,135 feet (1870 m). Despite its altitude, the area is indeed, as its name implies, a swamp. Saiwa Swamp National Park was created to protect the rare Sitatunga, an amphibious antelope living within the swamp's bushrushes and sedges. Colobus, Vervet, and Brazza monkeys; otters; giant forest squirrels; and water birds also dwell within the protected area. After cycling to the park entrance, trails and wooden platforms over the bogs lead to 'treehouses.' These are viewing platforms where visitors, sitting in tall trees, literally have a bird's-eye view over the swamp's flying, leaping, and stalking inhabitants.

Rating: Easy

Distance: 16–25 miles (27–42 km)

Terrain: Flat

Road Conditions: Paved, dirt track; low traffic

Sidetrip and Walk: Kitale Museum and Nature Trail

Accommodation and Meals:
° See Northwest Kenya Loop 1 Options.
° Saiwa Swamp: Camping; no food or drinks available
° Kipsain: Basic food supplies

Starting Point: Sirikwa Safari Guesthouse and Camp

The Kongoni, or hartebeest, is a plains animal frequently seen along the roadside by cyclists.

Route Directions: Cycle south on A1 5 miles (8 km). Turn left at the sign *Saiwa Swamp National Park*. A herbalist-doctor lives on the right should you wish to try local remedies for any illnesses.

Continue along this dirt road 0.5 miles (1 km) to Kipsain trading center. 2.5 miles (4 km) further is Saiwa Swamp Park Gate. Ask Rangers to store bikes while walking through the park.

Backtrack to A1. Either turn right and return to Sirikwa Safari Guesthouse and Camp or turn left and cycle nine miles to Kitale.

☐ **Sidetrip and Walk:** Kitale Museum is well worth a visit. Spend time in the hall featuring clothes, utensils, weapons, and jewelry from many tribes.

Walk the Nature Trail behind the Museum where a selection of trees are identified. Benches are placed in an opening where Golden Ibis, less common than Hadada and Sacred Ibis, are often seen and the trees resound with their hearty calls.

Northwest Kenya Loop 3
Mt. Elgon's Forests, Wildlife, and Hot Springs

Description: Mt. Elgon straddles Kenya's western border with Uganda. This massive volcano burst out of the Trans-Nzoia plains 15 million years ago. Today, the Kenya-Uganda border cuts through the center of the crater, leaving Wagagai, the highest peak (14,176 feet, 4,321 m), on the Ugandan side. Kenya claims two other peaks, Sudek (14,140 feet, 4,310 m) and Koitobos (13,882 feet, 4231 m). The immensity of the mountain, combined with the fact that its highest point is quite indistinguishable, makes for the commonly heard joke among locals: "Did you climb Mt. Elgon today?" one climber will ask. "Gee, I really don't know!" is the usual reply.

Masai call the mountain, *Ol Doinyo Igoon* meaning the 'Mountain of the Breast.' A remnant clan of Masai known as the il-Kong still lives near the mountain. Within Mt. Elgon National Park live bushbuck, duiker, elephant, and buffalo. Exploring forests, lava-tube caves, and a huge crater with hot springs are some of the area's attractions. Only one approach into this park is possible without a car, and that is through Kimilili. Foot safaris within this unspoiled and seldom-visited park are great adventures.

Rating: Challenger

Distance: 72 miles (120 km) roundtrip

Terrain: Hilly

Road Conditions: Paved, dirt tracks; low traffic.**Walks:**
- Walks through Kimilili Forest or Chepkitale Forest, often taking elephant trails.
- Climbing any or all of Mt. Elgon's peaks [Without Ugandan visas, it is advisable to stay on the Kenyan side of the crater.]

Accommodation and Meals:
- Kimilili: Basic lodges and *hotelis*.
- Chepkitale Forest Station: Basic hut [4 miles, (7 km) beyond the Forest Station]. Carry water from Kimilili or Kaberwa. Bring food supplies.
- Kitale: Return to Kitale's lodges for the night if you are not walking into the Forests.

Starting point: Kitale

Route Directions: Cycle south 31 miles (53 km) on A1 to Kimilili. [If coming from Kakamega (or any points south), cycle 50 miles (81 km) north on A1 to Kimilili].

From Kimilili continue 4.2 miles (7 km) to Kapsakwony. Keep left at the fork above this community.

Kimilili Forest Station is 2.7 miles (4.5 km) north of Kapsakwony. Check in with a Ranger before continuing. Decide whether to store bikes here and continue on foot, or ride on.

☐ **Walk:** A 12-mile (20 km) dirt road through dense bamboo forests leads to Chepkitale Forest Station. Shorter forest walks using elephant trails call forth every visual and auditory sense. Listen for those crashing sounds in the forests. Surprising elephant and especially buffalo is most unwise (see the section *Wildlife Dangers* in Chapter 9, *Wildlife In the Parks and Outside)*. 4 miles (7 km) beyond Chepkitale Forest Station is a simple hut with sleeping platforms.

☐ **Extended Walk:** Allow a minimum of 2–3 days to explore the crater and climb Elgon's peaks.

If backtracking to Kapsakwony under dry road conditions, take the minor road heading northeast. After 17 miles (28 km) this road rejoins A1 south of Kitale.

Northwest Kenya Loop 4
Kakamega Forest

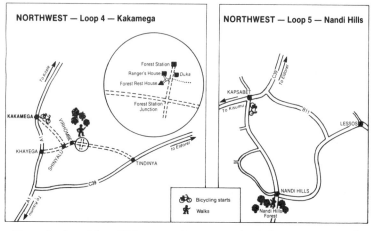

Description: Near Kakamega is a tract of rainforest separated from the rest of a once extensive West Africa forest by the drying up of the climate and the resulting replacement of trees by grasslands. This equatorial jungle survives as an isolated environment and home for many species of monkeys, birds, butterflies, and mammals, most found nowhere else in East Africa.

Within Kakamega Forest the only accommodation apart from camping is the Forest Rest House. This wooden building balanced on stilts is dubbed the 'Budget Treetops.' It has only four double rooms, each having a private bath and kerosene lantern (I had to furnish my own kerosene!). The caretaker's bird and animal walks are highly informative and entertaining. He 'talks' to the birds and monkeys who appear to listen intently and respond in similar 'language.' Hornbill, great blue turacos, grey parrots as well as blue, red-tail, and colobus monkeys are only a few of the delights to be seen while cycling or walking through Kakamega Forest. Enjoy a lingering remnant of Paradise.

Rating: Easy

Distance: 15 miles (25 km) each way

Terrain: Flat

Road Conditions: Mostly dirt tracks, some paved; low traffic

Sidetrip and Walks: Trails to small villages cut through the forest in many directions near the Forest Rest House. This is a peaceful, rural place. Cycle and walk as far as time allows.
- Guided bird and animal viewing walks with the Caretaker near Forest Rest House.
- Cycle to Nandiland via a backroad near the Forest Rest House.

Accommodation and Meals:
- Kakamega Forest: Forest Rest House (budget rooms or camping, no restaurant) For reservations, write The Forester, Box 88, Kakamega, Kenya.
- Kakamega: Golf Hotel (expensive rooms and restaurant) Kakamega Wayside House (budget rooms and restaurant)
- Bendera 85 (budget rooms and restaurant)

Starting Point: Kakamega's Approved School

Route Directions: Cycle the dirt road immediately beyond the school toward Shinyalu trading center. (Buy food supplies here if spending the night in the forest).

Turn left at the sign indicating the Forest. Continue three miles (5 km) to the Forest Rest House.

Alternately, if cycling from the south towards Kakamega town, turn right at the Forest sign six miles (10 km) before reaching Kakamega town. Continue 4.2 miles (7 km) to Shinyalu. From Shinyalu, follow the directions above.

☐ **Walks:** At the Forest Rest House, arrange for a guided morning or evening Forest walk with the Caretaker. Negotiate a fee in advance. Wandering through the forest unaccompanied is certainly an option, but with the Caretaker's assistance much more is seen and learned. Alternately, walk to a hill offering a good view of the entire area. The Caretaker can point out the trail.
Backtrack to Kakamega town.

☐ **Sidetrip:** A dirt track heading east from the Forest Rest House connects with the highway to Kapsabet after 15 miles (25 km). Get directions to this road from the Caretaker if visiting Nandiland is your next destination (see *Northwest Kenya Loop 5*, below).

Northwest Kenya Loop 5
Nandi Hills

Description: For quiet, peaceful cycling through a rural won-
derland, the Nandi Hills are difficult to surpass. Nandi tribesmen were formerly the fiercest opponents of the British. Today
they are traditional pastoralists and skillful cattle farmers. Tea
and sugarcane compose the region's major crops while Nandi
cattle produce more milk than any other district in Kenya. The
brilliant red Nandi Flame Trees seen throughout Kenya are
named after this place. Keep a sharp eye out for Chemoset, the
Nandi Bear who purportedly roams the high forests of the
Nandi Hills.

Rating: Challenger

Distance: 32 miles (53 km)

Terrain: Hilly

Road Conditions: Paved; low traffic

Sidetrips and Walks:
- Cycling north to Eldoret or the woodlands of Kaptagat
- Walking safaris in the Nandi Hills (See *Grand Tour;
  Northwest Kenya and Cherangani Hills* in Chapter 18 for
  hiking suggestions in the Nandi Hills)

Accommodation and Meals:
- Kapsabet: Kapsabet Hotel (budget rooms and restaurant)
- Eldoret: Sirikwa Hotel (moderate rooms and restaurant)
- Kaptagat: Kaptagat Hotel (budget rooms and restaurant)

Starting Point: Kapsabet. Cycle 11 miles (18 km) south to
the district capital, Nandi Hills.

☐ **Walk:** Walks into the forests and through highland communities of the Nandi Hills are refreshingly peaceful.
Ask the local Chief for a guide. If he and the assistant
chief are absent, inquire at the petrol station or hospital.
(Remember, the reason for seeking a guide is not because
you are an inept trail-finder: being accompanied by a
local has many advantages. Review the section *Using
Guides* in Chapter 8, *Getting Along with the Locals*).

Leave Nandi Hills via the road east which, after three miles
(5 km), bends northwards.

Coffee, tea, and sisal are Kenya's three largest export crops. A load of sisal is being carried to market on a mamba. *Meanwhile, the large sisal plantations are being phased out.*

After 7 miles (12 km) this road connects with the main Lessos–Kapsabet highway. Turn left on this highway (low traffic), returning to Kapsabet in 11 miles (18 km).

☐ **Sidetrip:** From Kapsabet cycle 25 miles (42 km) north to Eldoret, then 12 miles (20 km) east to the Kaptagat Hotel, a small establishment in a delightful forest. Camping by the stream is allowed.

CHAPTER 19

The Coast, North and South

Kenya's Coast extends 300 miles (480 km) from Somalia in the north to Tanzania in the south. White sand beaches and one of the world's most beautiful coral reefs are its star attractions. There is much more to enjoy along the Coast as cyclists and walkers quickly discover.

Coastal culture was influenced by Arabic and Asian traders and Portuguese. As these cultures intermarried, a distinct civilization called Swahili emerged. Ancient cities, whose ruins today are found along the Coast, are visible remains of this cultural blend. During the early nineteenth century when the Sultan of Oman ruled the Coast, Arabs flocked to East Africa, trading largely in slaves. When the British abolished slavery in 1907, freed people also became part of the Swahili society.

Mijikenda people make up nine coastal tribes: the Giriama, Digo, Rabai, Ribe, Duruma, Chonyi, Jibana, Kauma, and Kambe. Each tribe builds a central settlement some distance from the coast in which is placed a charm (called a fingo) attended by several elders. Like many Kenyan tribes, they adhere to age-set systems whereby young people gradually advance into different stages of adult responsibilities. Their ancient beliefs in spirits and ancestral powers are still adhered to today.

The Indian Ocean's crystal clear waters and enormous variety of tropical fish are punctuated by occasional channels, referred to in Kenya as 'creeks.' Boat trips along these creeks, which often cut several miles into coastal lands, are superb birdwatching excursions. Takaungu Creek is my personal favorite. Boats are available for hire just below the small fish market and ancient Arab tombs in Takaunga.

After snorkeling, diving, fishing, and boating, survey the variety of colorful flowering trees growing in the coastal region. Palm and mangoes wave gracefully while bright bougainvillaea, oleander, and hibiscus create a dazzling earthen rainbow. Frangipani is a tree with brilliant red blossoms, especially beautiful in May.

Ruined cities and mosques built by Arab Sultanates from about AD 900 onwards dot the coastline. Near Tiwi Beach on the south side of Mwachema River estuary, for example, is a well-preserved Persian mosque surrounded by giant baobob trees. A short distance north of Mombasa's Nyali Bridge, is Mtwapa's Nyumba la Mtwana ('the slave master's house'), an archaeological site boasting a fifteenth-century mosque and Arab pillar tomb. Don't miss the large pillar tomb in Malindi next to the mosque by the sea.

Gedi, only 10 miles (17 km) south of Malindi, is a larger fifteenth-century Arab city whose ruins were excavated from the jungle. While walking in the surrounding Jilore Forest Reserve, you may spot the unique golden-rumped shrew, an ancestor of the elephant.

In the far north of Kenya, only 60 miles south of Somalia, lies Lamu, the largest surviving city of the 1,000-year Arab civilization. The Swahili *Lamu Chronicle* records Lamu's found-

Cycling to Shimoni on Kenya's south coast, the author met this traveling salesman with an entire store aboard his bicycle. He is negotiating the sale of kangas, the rectangular pieces of cloth worn by local women.

ing in the seventh century, though nothing further is known of the city until 1402. During the sixteenth to nineteenth centuries the island town flourished. As it was eclipsed in importance by Mombasa and Zanzibar, Lamu retained its unique Afro-Arabic culture and today is a living museum. The celebration of the Prophet Mohammed's birthday, the largest and best-known Muslim festival in East Africa, occurs on the island in late October.

Lamu's old houses, built with two-foot thick coral walls, climb to three stories high. Their flat roofs provide popular sleeping and entertainment space for the community's residents. Manda Island is opposite the ancient city and Pate Island is only a short cruise away in a canvas-sail dhow.

At the southern tip of Kenya's Coast is Shimoni, a sleepy Swahili village. The first permanent British settlement on Kenya's mainland was here and remains of the District Officer's quarters, overgrown with greenery, crumble in the town square. Shimoni means 'place of the hole,' a reference to the nine-mile (15 km) long cave where slaves were retained. Dhows carry visitors past lovely islands to Kisite National Marine Park. While snorkeling you may emerge from the coral gardens, as I did, to witness the disappearance of tiny Kisite Island under the sea's waters, an especially distressful situation if you have left your beach clothes on the island.

Green and cool Shimba Hills provide a mountain refuge from the Coast's sometimes sweltering heat. The town of Kwale, surrounded by forest, is situated a short distance from Shimba Hills National Reserve Gate. The adventure of walking in these hills is enhanced by roaming forest elephant, buffalo, and many other animals. Indeed, elephant occasionally wander into the streets of Kwale. (Imagine this conversation overhead in Kwale: "Excuse me, sir. I can't leave your store because an elephant is blocking the door.") Check with local rangers for advice about which hills are safe for walking and whether an armed ranger guide is advisable. Wild animals move unpredictably, so getting a current update on their whereabouts is important.

Coastal Grand Tour:
Between Nairobi and Mombasa

Cycling the Nairobi–Mombasa highway is not safe, although undoubtedly some will disagree. The highway between Mombasa Harbor and Kenya's interior is too narrow in places to accommodate passing trucks and a cyclist. Since this thoroughfare is bordered on both sides by Tsavo East and West National Parks and several mountain ranges, finding sideroads for the entire 300-mile journey is impossible.

Traveling between Nairobi and the Coast on the historic 'Lunatic Express' is highly recommended. Try to book the 5:00 pm train which passes through Nairobi National Park before dark. If time allows for backroad cycling between Nairobi and Mombasa, use buses to reach the towns where these scenic routes begin:

☐ From Mtito Andei, cycle the dirt road towards Amboseli National Park. Views of wild animals and Mt. Kilimanjaro's crater rim are this backroad's rewards.

☐ From Voi, cycle Taveta Rd. to Taita Hills Lodge. From there, book an overnight stay at Salt Lick Lodge or a drive through the private animal sanctuary. Cycling further to Taveta near the Tanzanian border is an extended option.

☐ **Walks and Excursions:**
∘ In the Taita Hills, inhabited by friendly Taita people, walkers sometimes discover semi-precious stones. Inquire at Taita Hills Lodge for a guide into these steep hills.
∘ From Taveta (a train travels between Voi and Taveta), ride west to Lake Chala, a circular crater lake with inviting, cool water. Beware, however; I was told after a refreshing swim that crocodiles live in the lake, which is true.
∘ A longer ride eastwards from Taveta, in Kilimanjaro's shadow, skirts Lake Jipe's shores. After passing through small fishing villages, an unpretentious Tsavo West National Park Gate is reached. *Bandas* and campsites are only a few yards away. Lake Jipe's shoreline is usually crowded with elephant, hippo, and water birds making this end of Tsavo West National Park definitely worth a visit. The Lake Jipe Lodge offers superb accommodation, dining, and bar under the capable management of Mr. Ghandi. Alternately, ask rangers whether camping by the lake is possible.

191

North Coast Grand Tour

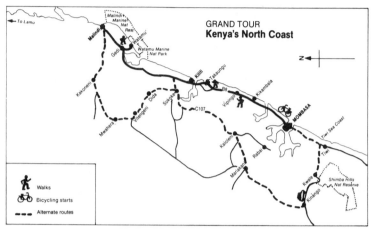

Starting Point: Mombasa. Before cycling north, see *Coast Loop 1* for a cycling or walking tour of Mombasa's Old Town.

Route Directions: Leaving Mombasa, cross the Nyali Bridge to the north using the bicycle lane. Follow *North Coast Loop 2* to Kikambala.

From Kikambala, follow B8 (known as Mombasa/Malindi Highway) north 9 miles (15 km) to Vipingo, a small trading center on the right.

See *North Coast Loop 3* for walks and sidetrips in the nearby coastal area including a farm by the sea.

Continue north on B8 from Vipingo 7 miles (12 km) to the sign, D552 indicating a right turn to Takaungu.

See *North Coast Loop 4* which describes a shortcut to Kilifi ferry.

Alternately, reach Kilifi ferry in 5.5 miles (9km) by remaining on B8 north. Cross to the north side of Kilifi Creek via the ferry (Japanese are building a bridge over Kilifi Creek, a project dragging on for years). Either take *North Coast Loop 5* to tour Kilifi Creek or continue north, through Kilifi trading center, another 26 miles (44 km) to a Gedi sign. This also signals the right turn leading to Watamu trading center and the Watamu Marine Park. See *North Coast Loop 6*.

Via the main highway Malindi is another 9 miles (15 km) further north.

Accommodation in Malindi:
- Silver Sands Campground (budget *bandas,* camping, dining)
- Driftwood Lodge (moderate rooms and dining)
- Scorpio Villas (moderate cottages with private cooks supplied upon request)

☐ **Sidetrip and Walk:** Lamu is 138 miles (236 km) north of Malindi. A hot, rough road connects these two towns. Flying from Malindi, if affordable, is a splendid option because aerial views of the coastline are breathtaking. The bus is a cheaper option and perhaps the only transport for bicycles to Lamu, apart from private vehicles. (The small aircraft used can scarcely accommodate hand luggage).
Lamu is a fine locale for cycling and walking since no cars are allowed. Donkeys are usually to blame for any 'traffic jams' on the island, as they wander everywhere. From Malindi consider several choices for the return trip to Mombasa: (a) backtrack cycling, (b) fly (Kenya Airways accommodates bicycles), (c) via bus, or (d) take the longer cycling sidetrip bypassing B8 highway. This route is strictly backroad cycling and best undertaken when roads are dry.

☐ **Sidetrip:** (for dry road conditions) Cycle west from Malindi to Kakoneni. Distance 18 miles (30 km). Continue 4.5 miles (8 km). Turn south to Mwahera (10.5 miles, 18 km), Vitengeni (8.5 miles, 14 km), and Dide (7.5 miles, 12 km), either returning to the main highway at the Kilifi Ferry in 21 miles (35 km) or connecting with C107 south at Sokoke (13 miles, 22 km). If opting for C107, continue south 31 miles (52 km) to Kaloleni. The busy Nairobi-Mombasa highway is crossed after 12 miles (20 km). C107 extends 30 miles (50 km) to Kinango. [East of Kinango are Kwale and Shimba Hills. Cycling from Kinango to Kwale is doubtful since the road crosses a section of Shimba Hills Reserve.] Take the bus to Kwale instead. See *South Coast Loop 7.*

South Coast Grand Tour

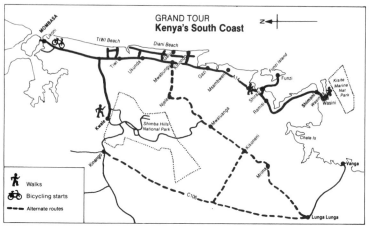

Starting Point: Mombasa. Board the Likoni Ferry to leave Mombasa Island and to reach the South Coast.

Route Directions: Cycle south on A14 (called the South Coast Highway). First left turn leads to Shelly Beach where the Shelly Beach Hotel offers moderately priced rooms and dining.

Continue south 9 miles (15 km) to the sign, Kwale, indicating a right turn for the 13-mile (23 km) sidetrip to Shimba Hills. See *South Coast Loop 7*. Stay on A14 south 2 miles (3 km) further to the sign, Tiwi Sea Coast, on the left.

Accommodation at Tiwi Sea Coast:
° Twiga Lodge (budget rooms, camping, and restaurant) Coral Cove Cottages, and Tiwi Villas (moderately priced cottages)

Backtrack to A14. Cycle south 4 miles (7 km) to a sign marking the left turn to Diani Beach and Ukunda trading center.

□ **Sidetrip:** Diani Beach is the most developed community of the South Coast. Posh tourist hotels line the beach offering excellent dining, dancing, sailing, and surfing.

To reach Diani Beach, turn left at the signpost on A14. After 1.5 miles (2.5 km) a T-junction is reached. This is Diani Beach Highway, which connects all hotels along this coastal strip. Turn right to Diani Beach Shopping Centre where two bicycle rental shops are located. Continue south 1 mile (2 km), to Ali Barbour's Restaurant serving gourmet cuisine in a cave. Further south 1 mile (2 km) Nomad's has a good beach bar and cottages to rent. Leaving Diani Beach, return to A14, the South Coast Highway.

Cycle south on A14 towards Shimoni. See *South Coast Loop 8* for directions to Shimoni, Sidetrips, and Walks to Swahili villages and South Coast islands. Return to Mombasa from Shimoni by following one of the options in *South Coast Loop 8*.

North and South Coast Loop 1
Mombasa City Tour

Description: Mombasa is Kenya's second largest city, but a prevailing Swahili atmosphere makes it look and feel almost nothing like Nairobi. The city is actually an island which was visited by Phoenician sailors circumnavigating Africa in 500 BC. After Vasco de Gama's visit in 1498, Portuguese occupied the island until routed by the Arabs in the eighteenth century. In Old Town Mombasa, structures built by Kenya's earliest foreign inhabitants survive. Houses with elaborately carved balconies line narrow streets between Makadara Rd. and the Old Harbor. Oriental mosques and temples are wedged between shops selling sweetmeats and long-necked copper pots. When night descends upon Old Town, aromatic, steaming, Arabic coffee is served from street corner stalls.

Considering the heavy traffic and short distance of this tour, walking through Old Town probably makes more sense than cycling.

Rating: Easy

Distance: 3 miles (5 km)

Terrain: Flat

Road Conditions: Paved, moderate traffic

Sidetrip and Walk:
- Walking tour of Old Town Mombasa
- Cycling Mombasa Island's coastline

Accommodation and Meals:
- Castle Hotel: (expensive rooms and restaurant)
- New Palm Tree (moderate rooms and restaurant)
- Lotus Hotel (moderate rooms and restaurant)
- Glory Guest House (budget rooms)
- Tamarind Restaurant (acclaimed Kenya's finest)
- Anglo-Swiss Bakery (moderate snacks and lunches)

Starting Point: Castle Hotel

Route Directions: Walk northeast along Nkrumah Rd. towards the sea. After passing Treasury Square with its monuments, Ft. Jesus is ahead. This fort's museum explains the Portuguese influence in Mombasa. Beneath the battlements, a footpath leads to a beach where fishermen cast their nets.

Nkrumah Rd. becomes Mbarak Hinawi Rd. leading to Government Square and the Customs Landing Stage. Dhows plying coastal waters to Lamu and beyond dock here. Surrounding Government Square are shops that sell carpets, carvings, chests, and brasswork.

A cliff to the west of Government Square has steps leading to a cave with a well where slaving dhows of bygone days secretly took on water.

Walk away from the sea, towards the modern city center, along Old Kilindini Rd. When you reach Digo Rd., turn right to City Market where spices, baskets, jewelry, and other goods are sold. Bargain tenaciously: This is largely the fun of shopping in Kenya's markets. City Market is bordered on the north by Biashara St. where fabrics and Moslem caps called *kofias* are sold.

Continue west on Biashara to Jomo Kenyatta Ave. Further west off Kenyatta Ave. is Mwembe Tayari, an African market selling witchdoctoring supplies.

Return to the Castle Hotel by walking northeast along Haile Selassie or Nkrumah Rd.

☐ **Sidetrip:** Cycle Mombasa's coastline. Head south on Digo Rd. from the Castle Hotel. Upon reaching the sea, turn left at the Baobob Forest into Mama Ngina Drive. Follow this road bordering the sea until it ends at Kimathi Ave. Turn left at Kimathi Ave. Then turn right into Digo Rd. Straight ahead is the Castle Hotel.

North Coast Loop 2
Beaches, Wildlife, Ancient Ruins:
Sightseeing North of Mombasa

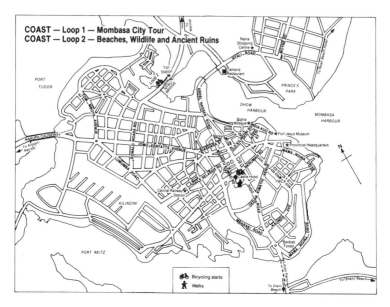

Description: Many sightseeing attractions are found along the North Coast only a few miles from Mombasa's city center. Bamburi's Nature Trail featuring a crocodile farm and other wildlife, Bombolulu's handicraft school offering fashionable jewelry and clothes made by handicapped students, the ancient Swahili ruins of Jumba La Mtwana, and lovely white sand beaches are all best explored on bicycle and foot. Access to the North Coast from Mombasa is via the Nyali Bridge.

Rating: Easy

Distance: 24 miles (40 km)

Terrain: Flat

Road Conditions: Paved, moderate traffic

Sidetrips and Walks:
- Horse riding along the beach leaving from Mamba Village.
- Beach-walk near the old and stately Nyali Beach Hotel.
- Walk the Bamburi Nature Trail.

∘ Cycle to Bombolulu Handicrafts Center.

Accommodation and Meals:
∘ Nyali Beach Hotel (expensive rooms and restaurant)
∘ Bamburi Beach Hotel (moderate rooms and restaurant)
∘ Kanamai Conference and Holiday Centre (budget rooms, cottages, camping and restaurant)

Starting Point: Mombasa's Nyali Bridge

Route Directions: Cross the bridge, using the bicycle lane, heading north. Turn right at the first stoplight. In 0.5 miles, (0.8 km) Ratna Fitness and Shopping Centre is on the left. Tamarind Restaurant, to the right, offers superb dining for big spenders. Continue straight to the beach road. Keep left, following the beach road, until you get to Nyali Beach Hotel.

☐ **Walk:** A footpath beside the hotel leads to the beach and miles of white-sand walking.

Leaving Nyali Beach Hotel, turn right. After 2 miles (3 km) the sign for Mamba Village signals a right turn. Mamba Villa is a tourist place, but if you are hankering for crocodile steak....

☐ **Sidetrip:** Horserides along the beach leave from Mamba Village.

Continue north from Mamba Village 2 miles (3 km) to an intersection joining B8 (called the Malindi/Mombasa Rd). [Flamboyant Bicycle Hire and Rides is located in the Birgis Complex at this intersection.]

☐ **Sidetrip:** From this intersection turn left onto B8 and continue 2 miles (3.5 km) to Bombolulu. Their jewelry is attractive, reasonably-priced, and purchases help the handicapped.

Turn right onto B8. Cycle 1 mile (2 km) to Bamburi Nature Trail. Admission is charged.

☐ **Walk:** Bamburi Nature Trail leads through an area of wild animals and exotic plants. In 1971 the Bamburi Cement Company embarked on an unique project to recreate a living environment on the vast lunar landscape of its quarry.

Leaving Bamburi Nature Trail, continue north 1.8 miles (3 km) to the toll booth. Beyond Mtwapa Bridge is a sign *Jumba La Mtwana*. Turn right and cycle 1.8 miles (3 km) to the beach where ruins of this fourteenth-fifteenth century Swahili community are found. This is an excellent picnic site.

Backtrack to B8. Either turn left to reach Mombasa by continuing straight on B8 or turn right, cycling north several miles to the sign *Kikambala–Kanamai Conference and Holiday Centre*. Look sharp: this sign is easily missed. Turn right onto a dirt road leading to the beach and the Centre.

North Coast Loop 3
A Farm by the Sea, Exploring Coral Reefs

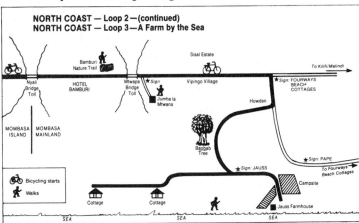

Description: Cycling to the Jauss Farm provides a chance to enjoy beautiful Indian Ocean beaches away from tourist hotels and crowds. This producing dairy farm, owned and managed by Mrs. Jauss, has a farmhouse, campground, and several guest cottages perched on cliffs overlooking the sea. Footpaths lead to a white sand beach and, when the tide is out, a walk to the coral reef reveals the underwater world of animals and plants.

Finding fresh fish for dinner is *hakuna matata* (no problem) since fishermen bring their catch directly from the sea to the farmhouse door. Homemade yogurt, cottage cheese, bread, and cakes are always available to purchase from the farmhouse kitchen. Recently Mrs. Jauss expanded what formerly was a limited camping facility. Now with an improved camping area (with showers), a small store, and cafe, the farm can accommodate larger groups. Let's hope the peaceful charm of Jauss farm remains.

Rating: Easy

Distance: 11 miles (18 km)

Terrain: Flat

Road Conditions: Paved, dirt; low traffic

Accommodations and Meals:
- Fourways Beach Cottages (moderate rooms or cottages and restaurant)

201

∘ Jauss Farm (budget cottages, camping, and restaurant)

Starting Point: Vipingo, located 19 miles (32 km) north of Mombasa.

Route Description: Cycle north from Vipingo village 1 mile (1.6 km) to a cluster of signs on the right. One sign reads, Fourways Beach Cottages. Turn right.

Continue on the dirt road 0.8 mile (1.4 km) to the sign, Howden, nailed to a tree. Turn right onto a narrow dirt lane, passing huge baobob trees, which leads to the Jauss Farm. When this lane ends, keep left to the Jauss Farmhouse and Camp.

☐ **Walks:** Walk (or cycle) through the dairy farm that stretches away from the sea. When the tide is out, venture onto the coral reef wearing protective shoes.

Backtrack to the Howden sign. Turn right on the dirt road. Keep left at the sign, Pape, and continue another 0.6 mile (1 km) to Fourways Beach Cottages and Restaurant. Cycle another 2 miles (3.6 km) to a Giriama village.

☐ **Walk:** To visit this Giriama village, first ask an *mzee* (older person) for permission. Present a small *chai* gift or offer to buy the vegetables on sale. Straight ahead is B8, the Malindi–Mombasa Rd. Either turn left, returning to Vipingo trading center after 2.5 miles (4 km), or turn right, cycling north to Takaungu (see *North Coast Loop 4*, below).

North Coast Loop 4
Old Swahili Village, Takaungu: Where Creek Meets Sea

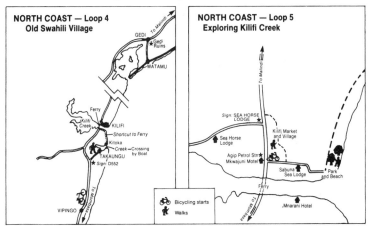

Description: Takaungu is the most delightful village I have discovered along Kenya's North Coast. It is an authentic Swahili community untainted by tourism. Residents are Arabic or Arabic-African in which case they refer to themselves as 'half-castes.' Situated at the confluence of a creek and the sea, the village boasts a beautiful, secluded beach on the Indian Ocean Coast and an inland channel bordered by dense tropical vegetation. Hidden within these tangled trees are small Digo settlements where singing and drum beating fill the night air. A shortcut to the Kilifi Ferry, much used by locals, starts on the other side of the creek, which is reached by canoe.

The Chief of Takaungu lives near the village shops. It is considered good manners to pay a visit if camping in Takaungu (see the section *Protocol: Meeting the Chief* in Chapter 8, *Getting Along with the Locals*). Takaungu is referred to in Karen Blixen's book, *Out of Africa*. It was to his home in Takaungu that Denys Finch-Hatton had flown before his fatal accident. Earlier, he had offered Karen his cottage by the sea in 'Takaunga' (her spelling):

"Denys sometimes talked of making Takaunga his home in Africa (…) When I began to talk of having to leave the farm, he offered me his house down there, as he had had mine in the highlands. But (…) Takaunga was too low and too hot for me."

Contrary to Ms. Blixen's decision, I would have taken the home in an instant. See if you do not agree.

Rating: Easy

Distance: 12 miles (20 km)

Terrain: Flat

Road Conditions: Paved/dirt; low traffic

Sidetrips and Walks:
° Walking tour of Takaungu.
° Explore the bird and animal life of Takaungu Creek by canoe.
° Walk to tribal villages at night when the dancing and singing have begun.

Accommodation and Meals:
° Takaungu: No lodges; camp on the beach or near the tombs overlooking the Creek.
° *Hotelis* sell delicious Swahili foods like chapatis, vibibis, mkates, halfcakes, and pink sweets made from the fruit of Baobob trees.
° Kilifi: Mkwajuni Hotel (budget rooms and restaurant).
° Sabuna Sea Lodge (moderate rooms and restaurant; see *North Coast Loop 5*).

Starting Point: Vipingo, 19 miles (32 km) north of Mombasa. [Buses from Mombasa going to Malindi pass here.]

This cyclist sets out to sell a load of sugarcane.

Route Directions: Cycle north on B8, Mombasa/Malindi Highway 7 miles (12 km) until the sign, D552, indicates a right turn to Takaungu.

Takaungu is reached after cycling 2.5 miles (4 km) on this graded dirt road.

☐ **Walk:** A walking tour of Takaungu starts with a stroll to the beach, visiting the secondary school along the way where the faculty includes one Peace Corps worker. Visit the Fish Market on a hill overlooking the confluence of creek and sea. Ask residents for directions to an ancient Indian Cemetery and the old village wells. Sit down to talk with people in the inner courtyards of homes where women are cooking various Swahili delicacies.

Leave Takaungu by crossing the Creek in a canoe provided for this purpose. Once on the other side, simply follow locals along the farm path to Kilifi Ferry. Complete this journey before dark.

North Coast Loop 5
Exploring Kilifi Creek

Description: Kilifi is best known as the place of the ferry crossing when traveling north to Malindi from Mombasa. After queuing several minutes or hours to board the ferry, most vehicle passengers race on to Watamu or Malindi. Few people linger to enjoy Kilifi Creek and town. After crossing to the north shore, a bicycle tour following the Creek to its confluence with the sea is refreshing, relaxing, and scenically very beautiful. At the road's end, a tree-filled park offers a shady picnicking site.

En route to the park, Giriama villages are interspersed with modern white villas. The contrasts are startling. It is dafe to swim or sunbathe on the beach fronting Sabuna Sea Lodge where non-residents of the hotel may also drink or dine. Bicycles can be rented at Sabuna Sea Lodge.

Rating: Easy

Distance: 12 miles (20 km)

Terrain: Flat

Road Conditions: Paved; low traffic

Accommodation and Meals:
- Kilifi, south side of Creek: Mnarani Hotel (expensive rooms and restaurant)
- Kilifi, north side of Creek: Mkwajuni Motel (budget rooms and restaurant)
- Sabuna Sea Lodge (moderate rooms and restaurant)
- Seahorse Lodge (expensive rooms and restaurant)

Starting Point: Kilifi, north shore.

Route Directions: Exiting the ferry, look for the sign, Sabuna Sea Lodge, on the right. Turn right at the sign and cycle 2.2 miles (3.6 km) to the Sabuna Sea Lodge.

Continue on the same road 2.4 miles (4 km) further. Stay on the road when it bends right and turn immediately left. After 1.3 miles (2.2 km) this road ends at the park where sea and creek meet.

☐ **Walk:** Explore the park, beach, and creek on foot.

Gazelle can be seen by the roadside in many parts of Kenya.

Backtrack to Kilifi village. Before reaching the highway, turn right to visit the Kilifi Market.

☐ **Sidetrip**: Return to B8. Cycle north from Kilifi town, passing the Mkwajuni Hotel. At the next intersection is the sign, Seahorse Lodge. Turn left at this sign and follow the hilly dirt road 1 mile (1.6 km) to Seahorse Lodge (operated by African Safari Club) bordering Kilifi Creek in an extremely private setting.

North Coast Loop 6
Gedi Ruins and Watamu Marine Park

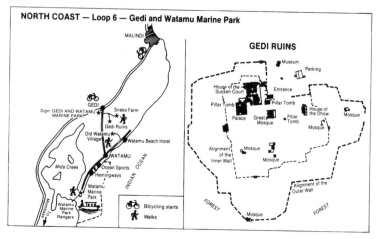

Description: Watamu used to be a sleepy little fishing village. The community is being developed now, though it still has a long way to go before rivaling the glut of tourist facilities at Diani Beach. Apart from some modern flats and homes, there is a small shopping center with hardware store, grocery, and Barclays Bank (open only three days/week). South of Watamu's trading center, only *dukas* and African villages line the roadside (with the one exception of an extravagant Catholic Church). Hemingway's and Ocean Sports Hotel are both on the seafront off the main road. The road ends at Watamu Marine Park's headquarters and, when cycling this direction, Mida Creek is on the right. Rangers at park headquarters provide boat trips along Mida Creek to observe its bird, monkey, and reptile life and to the coral gardens for snorkeling or diving (if diving, bring your own equipment). A fee is charged per boat.

Gedi's ruins are a bit eerie, but nevertheless captivating. A forest surrounding this old Swahili settlement is an exciting place to walk ... if the rustling sounds in the bush do not bother you. Nearby is a Giriama village evidencing too much familiarity with tourists. Its inhabitants want money to dance, and the whole scene seems a bit staged. Visit this village only if no other opportunities to meet Giriamas have come along. Gedi Museum is small but informative. If vipers interest you, down the road is a Snake Farm where admission is free.

Rating:	Easy	Challenger
Distance:	20.5 miles (34 km)	37 miles (62 km)
Terrain:	Flat	Gentle hills, flat

Road Conditions: Paved (a short dirt road leads to Gedi National Monument); low traffic

Sidetrips: Boat trip along Mida Creek
∘ Snorkeling or diving at the coral gardens of Watamu Marine Park
∘ Walk the Watamu Marine Park Headquarters's nature trail

Accommodation and Meals:
∘ Watamu-Ocean Sports Hotel (moderate rooms and restaurant)
∘ Hemingway's (expensive rooms and restaurant) Watamu Beach Hotel (expensive rooms and restaurant)
∘ Old Watumu village offers small budget inns and private rooms in locals' homes. Ask in the village.
∘ Adventist Youth Camp (camping)

Starting Point for Challenger Option: Malindi. From the Total Petrol Station roundabout, cycle south on B8, the Malindi — Mombasa Rd. After 8.5 miles (14 km) the sign, Gedi National Monument/Watamu Marine Park, marks the left turn to Watamu. From this intersection, follow the Easy Loop. After completing the Loop, backtrack to Malindi.

Starting Point for Easy Option: The intersection on B8 marked by the sign, Gedi National Monument/Watamu Marine Park.

Route Directions: Cycle east 0.5 miles (0.8 km) on the road to Watamu. Turn left into the trading center of Gedi. Continue 0.1 mile (0.2 km) further to a fork in the road. At this fork, the left road leads to the free Snake Farm. To the right is Gedi National Monument.

☐ **Walk:** Leave bikes at the entrance to Gedi while visiting the ruins and forest on foot. Buy the Guide pamphlet for 10 shillings. It offers intriguing data about this site.

Backtrack to the road leading to Watamu. Turn left towards Watamu and continue 3.5 miles (6 km), passing the Post Office, to a T-junction.

Turn left cycling past the supermarket and Watamu Cottages. After the Adventist Youth Camp, either turn right to modern Watamu Beach Hotel or turn left to the vastly more derelict and interesting old Watamu village.

Backtrack to the T-junction. Continue straight 1 mile (2 km) to the sign *Ocean Sports Hotel/Hemingway's*, indicating a left turn to both hotels.

☐ **Sidetrip:** Sportfishing, glassbottom boats, and snorkeling or diving trips to the coral gardens leave from Ocean Sports Hotel.

Further south a string of *dukas* appear on the left and Mida Creek on the right. In three miles (5 km) the road ends at Watamu Marine Park Headquarters.

☐ **Walk:** The Watamu Marine Park Headquarters's nature trail is an easy footpath meandering through bush where monkeys play. A small admission fee is charged.

☐ **Sidetrip:** Boats to Mida Creek and the coral gardens are available at Watamu Marine Park Headquarters. (I prefer boating to the Coral Gardens from here because the trip is longer and gives a more extensive view of the Coastline.) Backtrack to the T-junction. Turn left, returning to B8, the Mombasa–Malindi Road.

☐ **Challenger Option:** Cycle north to Malindi.

South Coast Loop 7
Cool and Refreshing Shimba Hills

Description: Shimba Hills is a cool and forested mountainous region rising 1,800 feet (555 m) above Tiwi Seacoast. From these hills, expansive views in all directions are possible. The surrounding forest reserve of 77 square miles (200 square km) is the only habitat of sable antelope in Kenya. Kwale, the district capital, is a small community which, at first glimpse, seems an undeveloped alpine resort. Beyond Kwale the road leading to the park gate of Shimba Hills National Reserve is heavily populated with elephant and buffalo. Cycling on the road beyond the village is, therefore, discouraged. For travel west of Kwale to Kinango, local buses or private transport are the best options.

Shimba Lodge was completed a few years ago and is rated as one of Kenya's finest. Advance reservations are necessary and, when booking accommodation, request to be picked up in Kwale by a lodge vehicle. The Lodge is within the Reserve, so cycling and walking to it are prohibited. It is unnecessary to stay overnight in Kwale since the downhill trip back to the beach takes little time. Cycling up the hills to reach Kwale is a good workout, but the rewards of cool air and low humidity make the ride worth the effort.

Rating: Challenger
[Easy Option: Flamboyant Bike Hire and Rides in the Diani Beach Shopping Centre leads evening rides to Shimba Hills. Participants are transported to Kwale where they begin the downhill ride. Alternately, take a local bus to Kwale, then cycle down.]

Distance: 22 miles (37 km)

Terrain: Hilly

Road Conditions: Paved; low traffic

Walk: Walking 'on the wild side' following elephant and buffalo trails through the Shimba Hills' forests

Accommodation and Meals:
° Shimba Hills National Reserve: Shimba Lodge (expensive rooms and dining: reservations in Mombasa, Tel. 471551, 471567/8; in Nairobi, Tel. 335807 FAX 254 2 543810)

° Kwale: Tonorokwa Lodge, next to the hospital (budget rooms), *hotelis* for dining

Starting Point: The Tiwi Seacoast exit on A14 (called South Coast Highway).

Route Directions: Cycle north 2 miles (3.6 km), using the paved sideroad on the east side of the highway, to the sign, Kwale C106.

Turn left onto the well-maintained paved road leading to Kwale. This climb is gentle for 6 miles (10 km) until you reach a small trading center.

☐ **Walk:** Stop to walk through the lovely grounds of the primary school on the left. This is a peaceful place to rest before tackling the steep climb ahead.

Continue 1 mile (2 km) further. Avoid taking the dirt road which forks to the left; it leads to one of the Reserve gates. After a long hill lasting 1.8 miles (3 km), Kwale is reached.

☐ **Walk:** Walks 'on the wild side' in the forests surrounding Kwale are highly adventurous. Before starting down an elephant trail, contact the warden in Kwale. He can recommend the safest trails to take into the forest since he is informed of recent buffalo and elephant sightings near the village. He may advise taking an armed Ranger-guide.

[To reach the North Coast from Kwale via backroads, take the bus to Kinango. Cycle north to Mariakani, bypassing Mombasa.]

Backtrack on C106 to Tiwi Seacoast.

☐ **Sidetrip:** When cycling downhill from Kwale towards the sea, after 7 miles (12 km), take the dirt road on the right. This road offers a different and more challenging route to Tiwi Seacoast.

South Coast Loop 8
Shimoni and Indian Ocean Islands

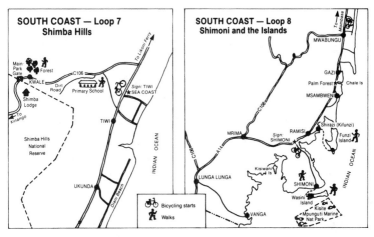

Description: Most tourists travel no further down the South Coast from Mombasa than Diani Beach where assorted enterprises vie for tourist business. Further south is a far more historically interesting region and Kenya's most beautiful marine park near Kisite Island. Other attractions include deep-sea fishing in Pemba Channel, which separates Kenya from Tanzania, and sailing to islands in traditional wooden dhows with canvas sails. For seafood dining extraordinaire, Wasini Island Restaurant prepares a feast no monarch would refuse. It lasts several hours during which eight different courses of fish are consumed. The restaurant's dhow collects passengers from the pier at Shimoni.

Between Shimoni and Diani Beach there are many Swahili villages to visit, untouched by tourism. At Msambweni, a seventeenth-century fishing village whose name means 'Place of the Antelope,' remains a pen which once incarcerated thousands of slaves. From here, during low tide, Funzi Island can be reached on foot. Few places you will ever cycle are so tropically idyllic as the 9 miles (15 km) leading to Shimoni village. Relax and enjoy.

Rating: Challenger (with Hardcore Extensions). [Easy Option: take the bus traveling south from Diani Beach or Mombasa. Ask to be let off at the Shimoni turn. Follow the tour from there, cycling 9 miles to the road's end at Shimoni.]

Distance: 32 miles (53 km) one way

Terrain: Flat

Road Conditions: Paved, dirt; low traffic

Sidetrips and Walks:
- Shimoni: Walk through the jungle to the coral caves where slaves were once kept.
- Walk along the seashore through baobob forests in the direction of Pemba Channel Fishing Club.
- Dhow sailing to Wasini Island, Kisite Island Marine Park, or the longer safari to Pemba Island north of Zanzibar.

Accommodation and Meals:
- Wasini Island: (budget cottages, camping, and restaurant)
- Shimoni: Shimoni Reef Fishing Lodge (moderate rooms and restaurant)
- Funzi Island: camping (a resort currently under construction)

Starting Point: A14, the South Coast Highway at the Diani Beach exit.

Route Directions: Cycle south (direction Lunga Lunga) on A14. After 10 miles (18 km) a palm forest is entered. 3 miles (5 km) further Msambweni is reached.

☐ **Walk:** Walk to Funzi Island at low tide. Fish, camp, or just stroll. Continue 8 miles (13 km) south to Shirazi or Kifunzi, immediately before Ramisi.

☐ **Walk:** Any track through the sugar fields leads to the tiny old settlement of Shirazi or Kifunzi. Residents cut mangrove poles, fish, and garden in a tropical setting so perfect that moviemakers must have designed it.

Ride 2 miles (3 km) further south to the sign indicating a left turn to Shimoni.

☐ **Easy Option:** Join the tour here.

Cycling 9 miles (15 km) on the dirt road to Shimoni is pure pleasure. This backroad exudes an exotic tropical feeling with bamboo groves, overhanging trees, and chattering, clicking jungle sounds.

When the road ends at Shimoni, turn left to reach Shimoni Reef Fishing Lodge; turn right to Pemba Channel Fishing

Club; proceed straight ahead to the pier where dhows sailing to the islands dock.

☐ **Sidetrip and Walk:** Sail the short distance to Wasini Island in either a small dhow or the large Wasini Island Restaurant Dhow. A walking tour of Wasini Island reveals ancient mosques, Swahili ruins, and a fascinating coral garden that can be explored on foot when the tide is out.

☐ **Sidetrip:** Sailing to Kisite Island National Marine Park takes more than an hour each way. A large dhow leaves from Wasini and Shimoni Piers each morning at 9:00 am, provides snorkeling gear, and, after several hours at the coral gardens, sails to Wasini Island for a fish feast at Wasini Island Restaurant. The cost is around US $35–50 depending upon the exchange rate.

☐ **Walk:** Near Shimoni, finding the coral caves where slaves were kept generally requires a guide. Several advertise their services in Shimoni village. The caves are entered via a ladder; bring a flashlight if you plan to walk far into the caves.

Take the dirt track which passes Pemba Channel Fishing Club, a primary school (which you will likely want to visit), and a baobob forest.

☐ **Extended Sidetrip:** For those blessed with wanderlust and for whom time is *hakuna matata* (no problem), consider a sailing adventure to Pemba Island. Bicycles can also travel in the big wooden dhows. If you have time to spare after exploring Pemba by bicycle and on foot, there is always Zanzibar and Madagascar and....
Leaving Shimoni, backtrack to A14.

☐ **Easy Option:** Catch the bus to Diani Beach or Mombasa.

☐ **Challenger Option:** Backtrack to Diani Beach on A14.

☐ **Hardcore Extensions**: one of the following options:

☐ **Option**: Turn left. This 36-mile (61 km) route continues south 8.5 miles (14 km) until the right turn to Mrima. In 6 miles (10 km) Kikoneni is reached. Cycle straight on, through Njele, meeting A14 at Mwabungu. Turn left and cycle north on A14 to Diani Beach or Mombasa.

☐ **Option:** Follow the first option until you reach Kikoneni. Turn left onto the dry-season road to Mwanayamala. After 14 miles (23 km) is Mwangulu, at the western tip of Shimba Hills National Reserve. Cycle north on C106 15 miles (25 km) to Kinango. This option covers 44 miles (73 km). [Cycling to Kwale is discouraged because the road passes through the Shimba Hills Reserve. Bus to Kwale and follow *North Coast Loop 7* to reach A14 at the Tiwi Seacoast. Alternately, cycle north from Kanango on C107, crossing the Nairobi–Mombasa Highway, to Kilifi on Kenya's North Coast.]

☐ **Option:** Turn left on A14. Cycle south 21 miles (35 km) to Lunga Lunga. Take C106, an all-weather road, 9.5 miles (16 km) to Mwangulu. Continue north 24 miles (41 km) to Kinango. This last option covers 55 miles (92 km). Leave Kinango via the same routes outlined in the second option above.

Appendix A
Swahili for Active Travelers (Copy, trim, and fold to fit in wallet)

Hello, good-bey	*Jambo, kwaheri*
How are you?	*Habari?*
Where	*Wapi?*
Where is ...?	*Iko wapi?*
Why	*Kwa nini?*
How many/much	*Ngapi?*
I want ...	*Nataka ...?*
Please	*Tafahali*
Thanks a lot	*Asante sana*
Yes, no	*Ndiyo, hapana*
European (white)	*mzungu*
cold, hot	*baridi, moto*
tea, coffee	*chai, kahawa*
fish, meat	*samaki, nyama*
salt, pepper	*chumvi, pilipili*
sugar, milk	*sukali, maziwa*
saucepan, cup	*sufuria, kikombe*
matches, firewood	*kibiriti, kuni*
lamp, flashlight	*taa*
wine, beer	*divai, pombe*
banana, orange	*ndizi, chungwa*
tent, knife	*hema, kisu*
hut, path	*nyumba, njia*
wait, eat, give	*ngoja, kula, kupa*

half, one	*musu, moja*
two, three	*mgili, tatu*
four, five	*nne, tano*
six, seven	*sita, saba*
eight, nine	*nane, tisa*
ten, twenty	*kumi, ishirini*
thirty	*thelathini*
fifty, hundred	*hamsini, mia*
many, much	*mingi*
big, small	*kubwa, kidogo*
good, bad	*mzuri, mbaya*
black, white	*neusi, neupe*
far, near	*mbali, karibu*
bicycle	*baiskeli*
chain, pedal	*mnyororo, kanyagio*
brake	*kizuizi cha gari*
I want repairs	*Nataka matengenezo*
tube, patch	*mrija, kiraka*
repairman	*mfanya kazi*
workshop	*kiwanda cha kazi*
train, bus	*garimishi, basi*
car, taxi	*gari/motokaa, taksi*
shoes, pants	*kiatu, suruali*
gloves	*mfuko wa mkono*
I'm tired, sick	*nachoka, mgonjwa*
medicine, doctor	*dawa, daktari*

Appendix B
Swahili Sayings

Traditional ways of thinking are embodied in a country's proverbs. Situations encountered while cycling and walking through Kenya may be better understood if viewed through the perspective of these Swahili sayings. The Swahili is followed by the English translations of S. S. Farsi, *Swahili Sayings* (Kenya Literature Bureau, Nairobi).

Safety Precautions

Aliye kando haangukiwi na mti.
He who keeps to the roadside will have no tree fall on him.

Hasara humfika mwenye mabezo.
Loss befalls a careless fellow.

Kawia ufike.
Better delay and get there.

Wildlife In and Outside the Parks

Angurumap simba, Mcheza nani?
Who dares play when the lion roars?

Benefits of Cycling and Walking

Atangaye sana na jua, hujua.
He who wanders around a lot by day, he knows (because he learns a lot).

Mwenda bure si mkaa bure, huenda akaokota.
One who travels for no apparent purpose is not like one who sits down with no purpose — the traveler always picks up something.

Kipendacho moyo ni dawa.
A little of what the heart desires does you good!

Kipya kinyemi, ingawa kidonda.
A new thing is a source of joy even if it be a sore.

Mtembezi hula miguu yake.
An aimless wanderer wears away his legs, using up the energy in his legs to no good purpose.

Getting Along With the Locals

Hewalla! haigombi.
Civility does not cause disagreement.

Asiyeuliza, hanalo ajifunzalo.
He who does not ask questions has nothing to learn.

Kupanda Mchongoma, kushuka ndio ngoma.
You may do or say something in haste or anger, then find that getting out of the situation created is very difficult.

Mchama ago hanyeli, huenda akauya papo.
A traveler does not make a mess where he had made a camp as he might one day come back.

Ulimi unauma kuliko meno.
The tongue hurts more than the teeth.

Customs and Police Checkpoints

Usile na kipofu ukamgusa mkono.
When dealing with a simple person you must be very careful lest you might do something to make him suspicious of you.

Wema hauozi.
Kindness never goes bad.

Chai Gifts

Mgeni njoo mwenyeji apone.
Let a guest come, so that the host may benefit (it is usual for a guest to bring his/her host some gift).

Hakuna Matata, 'No Problem' Spirit

Haraka haraka haina baraka.
Hurry, hurry, has no blessing.

Mwenye pupa hadiriki kula tamu.
A hasty person misses the sweet things (because he cannot wait for the fruit to ripen).

Subira ni ufunguo wa faraja.
Patience is the key to tranquility.

Taratibu ndiyo mwendo
Slowly is indeed the way to walk.

Bibliography

Adamson, Joy. *Born Free*. New York: Scholastic Book Services, 1961.

Bradt, Hilary. *Backpacker's Africa*. Edison, New Jersey: Hunter Publishing, 1989.

Consolata Fathers. *Meru*. Turin, Italy: Poligrafico, Roggero & Tortia, 1988.

—. *Pokot*. Turin, Italy: Poligrafico, Roggero & Tortia, 1988.

Camerapix, ed. *Spectrum Guide to Kenya*. Nairobi: Westlands Sundries, 1989.

Cox, Thornton. *Traveller's Guide to East Africa*. New York: Hastings House Publishers, 1980.

Dinesen, Isak (ps. for Karen Blixen). *Out of Africa*. Alexandria, Virginia: Time-Life Books, 1965.

Else, David. *Camping Guide to Kenya*. Edison, New Jersey: Hunter Publishing, 1989.

Farsi, S. S. *Swahili Sayings*. Nairobi: Kenya Literature Bureau, 1988.

Hanby, Jeanette and David Bygott. *Kangas: 101 Uses*. Nairobi: Ines May Publicity, 1985.

Hargreaves, Dorothy and Bob. *African Blossoms*. Kailua, Hawaii: Hargreaves Company, 1972.

Heminway, John. No Man's Land, *The Last of White Africa*. San Diego: Harcourt Brace Javonovich, Publishers, 1983.

Huxley, Elspeth. *The Flame Trees of Thika*. New York: Viking Penguin, 1986.

—. *Out in the Midday Sun*. New York: Viking Penguin, 1985.

Jones, Eldred Durosimi, Eustace Palmer and Marjorie Jones, eds. *Women in African Literature Today*. Trenton, New Jersey: Africa World Press, 1987.

Karmali, John. *Beautiful Birds of Kenya*. Nairobi: Westlands Sundries, 1985.

Kipkorir, Benjamin. *Kenya's People: People of the Rift Valley*, Kalenjin. London: Evans Brothers, 1985.

Leakey, Richard E. *One Life*. Topsfield, Massachusettes: Salem House, 1986.

Livingstone, David. *Travels and Researches in South Africa*. London: The Amalgamated Pressa, 1905.

Macintyre, Kate. *The Nairobi Guide*. London: Macmillan Publishers, 1986.

Mackenzie, Jeanne. *Cycling*. New York: Oxford University Press, 1981.

Miller, Charles. *The Lunatic Express*. Nairobi: Westlands Sundries, 1987.

Moorehead, Alan. *The White Nile*. New York: Viking Penguin, 1972.

Moss, R.W. *Nairobi A to Z*. Nairobi: Kenway Publications, 1988.

Murphy, Dervla. *Full Tilt: Dunkirk to Delhi By Bicycle*. London: Century, 1989.

Njau, Rebeka and Gideon Mulaki. *Kenya Women Heroes and Their Mystical Power, Vol. I*. Nairobi: Risk Risk Publications, 1984.

Perrot, D.V. *Swahili Dictionary*. Kent, England: Hodder and Stoughton, 1988.

Place, James. *East African Explorers*. Nairobi: Oxford University Press, 1967.

Shales, Melissa, ed. *The Traveller's Handbook*. London: Wexas, 1988.

Sheldrick, Daphne. *The Orphans of Tsavo*. London: Collins and Harvill Press, 1968.

Trillo, Richard. *The Rough Guide to Kenya*. London: Harrap-Columbus, 1988.

Turner, Dr. Anthony C. *The Traveller's Health Guide*. London: Roger Lascelles, 1979.

Williams, J.G. *A Field Guide to the National Parks of East Africa*. London: William Collins & Co., 1988.

Wilson, Peter M. *Simplified Swahili*. Essex: Longman House, 1987.

Index